Words from George Harrison

Everybody is looking for KṚṢṆA.
Some don't realize that they are, but they are.
KṚṢṆA is GOD, the Source of all that exists,
the Cause of all that is, was, or ever will be.
As GOD is unlimited, HE has many Names.
Allah-Buddha-Jehova-Rāma:
All are KṚṢṆA, all are ONE.
By serving GOD through each thought, word, and
DEED, and by chanting of HIS Holy Names,
the devotee quickly develops God-consciousness.
By chanting
Hare Kṛṣṇa, Hare Kṛṣṇa
Kṛṣṇa Kṛṣṇa, Hare Hare
Hare Rāma, Hare Rāma
Rāma Rāma, Hare Hare

one inevitably arrives at KṚṢṆA Consciousness.
(The proof of the pudding is in the eating!)

ALL YOU NEED IS LOVE (KRISHNA) HARI BOL.
George Harrison

Books by His Divine Grace
A. C. Bhaktivedanta Swami Prabhupāda

Bhagavad-gītā As It Is
Śrīmad-Bhāgavatam (completed by disciples)
Śrī Caitanya-caritāmṛta
Kṛṣṇa, the Supreme Personality of Godhead
Teachings of Lord Caitanya
The Nectar of Devotion
The Nectar of Instruction
Śrī Īśopaniṣad
Light of the Bhāgavata
Easy Journey to Other Planets
Teachings of Lord Kapila, the Son of Devahūti
Teachings of Queen Kuntī
Message of Godhead
The Science of Self-Realization
The Perfection of Yoga
Beyond Birth and Death
On the Way to Kṛṣṇa
Rāja-vidyā: The King of Knowledge
Elevation to Kṛṣṇa Consciousness
Kṛṣṇa consciousness: The Matchless Gift
Kṛṣṇa consciousness: The Topmost Yoga System
Perfect Questions, Perfect Answers
Life Comes from Life
The Nārada-bhakti-sūtra (completed by disciples)
The Mukunda-mālā-stotra (completed by disciples)
Geetār-gān (Bengali)
Vairāgya-vidyā (Bengali)
Buddhi-yoga (Bengali)
Bhakti-ratna-boli (Bengali)
Back to Godhead magazine (founder)

Books compiled from the teachings of
Śrīla Prabhupāda after his lifetime

Search for Liberation
A Second Chance
The Journey of Self-Discovery
Civilization and Transcendence
The Laws of Nature
Renunciation Through Wisdom
The Quest for Enlightenment
Dharma, the Way of Transcendence
Beyond Illusion and Doubt
The Hare Kṛṣṇa Challenge

Available from krishna.com and blservices.com

CHANT
and be
HAPPY

THE POWER OF MANTRA MEDITATION

Based on the teachings of

His Divine Grace
A. C. Bhaktivedanta Swami
Prabhupāda

Founder-*Ācārya* of the International Society
for Krishna Consciousness

THE BHAKTIVEDANTA BOOK TRUST

Readers interested in the subject matter of
this book are invited by the International Society
for Krishna Consciousness to visit any
ISKCON center (see address list in back of book)
or to correspond with the Secretary at:

ISKCON Reader Services
P. O. Box 730, Watford, WD25 8ZE
United Kingdom
Tel: +44 (0)1923 857244
readerservices@pamho.net
www.iskconuk.com
www.krishnawisdom.com

BBT Africa
84 Tennyson Road, Lombardy East
2090, Johannesburg, South Africa
info@bbtafrica.co.za
www.bbtafrica.co.za
www.namahatta.co.za

FSC
www.fsc.org
MIX
Paper from
responsible sources
FSC® C006701

The ebook version of this title is available for free at
www.bbtmedia.com/en
Code: **EB16EN44368P**

ISBN 978-1-84599-088-6

www.krishna.com

Printed in 2014

We dedicate this book to our beloved
spiritual master and guide, His Divine Grace
A. C. Bhaktivedanta Swami Prabhupāda,
who brought the transcendental teachings of
Lord Kṛṣṇa, including the authorized science
of reincarnation, to the Western world.

The Editors

Contents

PREFACE

The Search for Happiness

Everyone wants to be happy. Some of us seek happiness through our families, in natural and healthy living, in successful careers, active social lives, fine gourmet foods, gambling, or through sports and exercise. Others experience happiness in politics, the arts, academia, or in hobbies ranging from mechanics and computer science to drama, philanthropy, welfare work, and literally thousands of other activities that comprise humankind's unending quest for pleasure. Millions of people find their happiness in liquor, mood elevators, tranquilizers, or other drugs.

Each day doctors and scientists discover more about how the human mind and body work. Yet with this abundance of scientific knowledge and space age technology, which vastly outstrips that of all previous generations, are modern people really any happier than their predecessors?

The basic problem in our search for happiness is that our sources of pleasure are all limited. What many people consider our most basic and fundamental pleasures – eating and sex – can only occupy a few moments of each day. Our bodies constantly thwart our plans for enjoyment. After all, you can only eat so much before becoming ill. Even sex has its limits.

Chant and Be Happy provides information about how we can expand our pleasure beyond our present limitations. It deals with a pleasure principle that operates beyond the bounds of time and space and emanates from the innermost part of our being. This book thoroughly explains how this inner happiness can be experienced immediately by anyone, through the mystical power of transcendental sound vibrations.

This technique for obtaining unlimited happiness does not depend on new products touted by Fleet Street whiz kids or Hollywood moguls, but has been successfully practiced by countless people throughout the ages. *Chant and Be Happy* explains how to use these transcendental sound vibrations to attain the ultimate state of happiness. It's an easy process, and it's free.

To achieve this unlimited and imperishable happiness one need only chant and hear what sages of ancient India have for millennia called the Great Chant for Deliverance, the Hare Kṛṣṇa *mahā-mantra*. This simple, sixteen-word mantra is comprised of sound vibrations powerful enough to awaken the natural happiness within everyone.

Hare Kṛṣṇa, Hare Kṛṣṇa, Kṛṣṇa Kṛṣṇa, Hare Hare
Hare Rāma, Hare Rāma, Rāma Rāma, Hare Hare

In recent years, millions have learned how to chant the Hare Kṛṣṇa mantra and experience this true, spiritual happiness. It is the most popular mantra in India, the homeland of meditation, and differs from other systems in two ways. First, the complete mantra is chanted (not just a fragment of a mantra) and second, the mantra is chanted aloud (not silently).

A brief introduction by His Divine Grace A. C. Bhaktivedanta Swami Prabhupāda, the founder and spiritual master of the International Society for Krishna Consciousness, explains the exact nature and meaning of the mantra. Chapter one, an exclusive interview with the late George Harrison, reveals how the Hare Kṛṣṇa mantra played a leading role in his life over the years. George explains that although he had achieved riches and fame beyond what most people could ever hope for, he found that there was "nothing higher" than the happiness he experienced from chanting Hare Kṛṣṇa. George discusses his confidence in the mantra's power over death, explains how much of his musical career was influenced by and intimately connected with the Hare Kṛṣṇa mantra, and describes the knowledge, bliss, and spiritual intelligence that comes from chanting.

In chapter two, Śrīla Prabhupāda speaks with John Lennon, Yoko Ono, and George Harrison at John's estate in Tittenhurst Park, discussing the potency of the Hare Kṛṣṇa mantra as the path to peace and liberation.

Chapter three is a fascinating account of how Śrīla Prabhupāda brought the chanting of Hare Kṛṣṇa from India to the Western world in the midst of the countercultural turmoil of the sixties and convinced the disillusioned hippies of New York's Greenwich Village and San Francisco's Haight-Ashbury that this mantra, not psychedelic drugs and antiwar protests, would make them happy. The history of chanting and meditating for higher consciousness is discussed in chapter four. The next chapter delineates the life and teachings of Śrī Caitanya Mahāprabhu, the sixteenth-century saint, mystic, and incarnation of Lord Kṛṣṇa who popularized the timeless practice of chanting the Hare Kṛṣṇa mantra.

Chapter six, a narration taken from one of India's

most important historical and philosophical literatures, the *Śrī Caitanya-caritāmṛta,* reveals how by simply hearing the chanting of Hare Kṛṣṇa from a genuine spiritual master anyone's character can be freed from all unwanted qualities.

The next chapter forms a treatise on self-realization, mantras, religion, and the power of the mind in meditation, compiled from the teachings presented in Śrīla Prabhupāda's books. Chapter eight explains the wide-ranging effects and personal benefits one can expect from chanting Hare Kṛṣṇa. The final chapter gives practical, step-by-step instructions for chanting, which if followed will open the door to ultimate happiness.

INTRODUCTION

On Chanting

Shortly after His Divine Grace A. C. Bhaktivedanta Swami Prabhupāda brought the Hare Kṛṣṇa mantra to the West in 1965, "Hare Kṛṣṇa" became a household word. In 1979, Dr. A. L. Basham, the world's leading authority on Indian history and religion, wrote of the Hare Kṛṣṇa movement, "It arose out of nothing in less than twenty years and has become known all over the West. This, I feel, is a sign of the times and an important fact in the history of the Western world."

But what exactly do the words "Hare Kṛṣṇa" mean? In this short essay from the album Krishna Consciousness, *which first introduced Beatles George Harrison and John Lennon to the chanting, Śrīla Prabhupāda explains the meaning of the Hare Kṛṣṇa mantra.*

The transcendental vibration established by the chanting of Hare Kṛṣṇa, Hare Kṛṣṇa, Kṛṣṇa Kṛṣṇa, Hare Hare/ Hare Rāma, Hare Rāma, Rāma Rāma, Hare Hare [Huh-ray; Krish-na; Rahm-uh] is the sublime method for reviving our transcendental consciousness.

As living spiritual souls, we are all originally Kṛṣṇa conscious entities, but due to our association with matter from time immemorial, our consciousness is now adulterated by the material atmosphere. The material atmosphere, in which we are now living, is called *māyā,* or illusion. *Māyā* means "that which is not." And what is this illusion? The illusion is that we are all trying to be lords of material nature, while actually we are under the grip of her stringent laws. When a servant artificially tries to imitate the all-powerful master, he is said to be in illusion. We are trying to exploit the resources of material nature, but actually we are becoming more and more entangled in her complexities. Therefore, although we are engaged in a hard struggle to conquer nature, we are ever more dependent on her. This illusory struggle against material nature can be stopped at once by revival of our eternal Kṛṣṇa consciousness.

Chanting Hare Kṛṣṇa, Hare Kṛṣṇa, Kṛṣṇa Kṛṣṇa, Hare Hare/ Hare Rāma, Hare Rāma, Rāma Rāma, Hare Hare is the transcendental process for reviving this original, pure consciousness. By chanting this transcendental vibration, we can cleanse away all misgivings within our hearts. The basic principle of all such misgivings is the false consciousness that I am the lord of all I survey.

Kṛṣṇa consciousness is not an artificial imposition on the mind. This consciousness is the original, natural energy of the living entity. When we hear this transcendental vibration, this consciousness is revived. This simplest method of meditation is recommended for this age. By practical experience also, one can perceive that by chanting this *mahā-mantra,* or the Great Chanting for Deliverance, one can at once feel transcendental ecstasy coming through from the spiritual stratum.

In the material concept of life we are busy in the matter of sense gratification, as if we were in the lower, animal stage. A little elevated from this status of sense gratification, one is engaged in mental speculation for the purpose of getting out of the material clutches. A little elevated from this speculative status, when one is intelligent enough, one tries to find out the supreme cause of all causes – within and without. And when one is factually on the plane of spiritual understanding, surpassing the stages of sense, mind, and intelligence, he is then on the transcendental plane. This chanting of the Hare Kṛṣṇa mantra is enacted from the spiritual platform, and thus this sound vibration surpasses all lower strata of consciousness – namely sensual, mental, and intellectual. There is no need, therefore, to understand the language of the mantra, nor is there any need for mental speculation nor any intellectual adjustment for chanting this *mahā-mantra*. It is automatic, coming from the spiritual platform, and as such, anyone can take part in the chanting without any previous qualification. Of course, in a more advanced stage of spiritual understanding, one is expected to avoid committing offenses.

But there is no doubt that chanting takes one immediately to the spiritual platform, and one shows the first symptom of this in the urge to dance along with the chanting of the mantra. We have seen this practically. Even a child can take part in the chanting and dancing. Of course, for one who is too entangled in material life, it takes a little more time, but even such a materially engrossed man is raised to the spiritual platform very quickly. When the mantra is chanted by a pure devotee of the Lord in love, it has the greatest efficacy on hearers, and as such this chanting should be heard from the lips of a pure devotee of the Lord, so that immediate effects can be achieved.

The word *Harā* is the form of addressing the energy of the Lord, and the words *Kṛṣṇa* and *Rāma* are forms of addressing the Lord Himself. Both *Kṛṣṇa* and *Rāma* mean "the supreme pleasure," and *Harā* is the supreme pleasure energy of the Lord, changed to *Hare* in the vocative. The supreme pleasure energy of the Lord helps us to reach the Lord.

The material energy, called *māyā,* is also one of the multi-energies of the Lord. And we, the living entities, are the marginal energy of the Lord. The living entities are described as superior to material energy. When the marginal energy is in contact with the inferior, material energy, an incompatible situation arises; but when the marginal energy is in contact with the superior energy Harā, it is established in its happy, normal condition.

These three words, namely *Hare, Kṛṣṇa,* and *Rāma,* are the transcendental seeds of the *mahā-mantra*. The chanting is a spiritual call for the Lord and His energy to give protection to the conditioned soul. This chanting is exactly like the genuine cry of a child for its mother. Mother Harā helps the devotee achieve the Supreme Father's grace, and the Lord reveals Himself to the devotee who chants this mantra sincerely.

No other means of spiritual realization is as effective in this age of quarrel and hypocrisy as the chanting of the *mahā-mantra:*

Hare Kṛṣṇa, Hare Kṛṣṇa, Kṛṣṇa Kṛṣṇa, Hare Hare
Hare Rāma, Hare Rāma, Rāma Rāma, Hare Hare

CHAPTER ONE

The Hare Kṛṣṇa Mantra: "There Is Nothing Higher . . ."

A 1982 interview with George Harrison

If you open up your heart
You will know what I mean
We've been polluted so long
But here's a way for you to get clean

By chanting the names of the Lord and you'll be free
The Lord is awaiting on you all to awaken and see

"Awaiting On You All"
from the album *All Things Must Pass*

In the summer of 1969, before the dissolution of the most popular music group of all time, George Harrison produced a hit single, "The Hare Krishna Mantra," performed by George and the members of the London Rādhā-Kṛṣṇa Temple. Soon after rising to the Top 10 or Top 20 best-selling record charts throughout England, Europe, and parts of Asia, the Hare Kṛṣṇa chant became a household word – especially in England, where the BBC had featured the Hare Kṛṣṇa Chanters, as they were then called, four times on the country's most popular television program, *Top of the Pops*.

At about the same time, five thousand miles away, several shaven-headed, saffron-robed men and sari-clad women sang along with John Lennon and Yoko Ono as they recorded the hit song "Give Peace a Chance" in their room at Montreal's Queen Elizabeth Hotel:

> *John and Yoko, Timmy Leary, Rosemary, Tommy Smothers,*
> *Bobby Dylan, Tommy Cooper, Derek Taylor, Norman*
> *Mailer, Allen Ginsberg, Hare Krishna, Hare Hare Krishna.*
> *All we are saying is give peace a chance.*

The Hare Kṛṣṇa devotees had been visiting with the Lennons for several days, discussing world peace and self-realization. Because of this and other widespread exposure, people all over the world soon began to identify the chanting Hare Kṛṣṇa devotees as harbingers of a more simple, joyful, peaceful way of life.

George Harrison was the impetus for the Beatles' spiritual quest of the sixties, and up until his death in 2001, the chanting of the Hare Kṛṣṇa *mahā-mantra* – Hare Kṛṣṇa, Hare Kṛṣṇa, Kṛṣṇa Kṛṣṇa, Hare Hare/ Hare Rāma, Hare Rāma, Rāma Rāma, Hare Hare – continued to play a key role in his life.

In this conversation with his long-time personal friend Contemporary Vedic Library Series editor Mukunda Goswami, taped at George's home in England on September 4, 1982, George reveals some of the memorable experiences he had chanting Hare Kṛṣṇa and describes in detail his deep personal realizations about the chanting. He explains what factors led him to produce "The Hare Krishna Mantra" record, "My Sweet Lord," and the LPs *All Things Must Pass* and *Living in the Material World* – all of which were influenced to a great extent by the Hare Kṛṣṇa chanting and philosophy. He speaks lovingly and openly of his association with His Divine Grace A. C. Bhaktivedanta Swami Prabhupāda, founder-*ācārya* of the Hare Kṛṣṇa movement. George also speaks frankly about his personal philosophy regarding the Hare Kṛṣṇa movement, music, yoga, reincarnation, karma, the soul, God, and Christianity. The conversation concludes with his fond remembrances of a visit to the birthplace of Lord Kṛṣṇa in Vṛndāvana, India, home of the Hare Kṛṣṇa mantra, and with George discussing some of his celebrity friends' involvement with the mantra now heard and chanted around the world.

Mukunda Goswami: Oftentimes you speak of yourself as a plainclothes devotee, a closet yogi or "closet Kṛṣṇa," and millions of people all over the world have been introduced to the chanting by your songs. But what about you? How did you first come in contact with Kṛṣṇa?
George Harrison: Through my visits to India. So by the time the Hare Kṛṣṇa movement first came to England in 1969, John and I had already gotten ahold of Prabhupāda's first album, *Kṛṣṇa Consciousness*. We had played it a lot and liked it. That was the first time I'd ever heard the chanting of the *mahā-mantra*.
Mukunda: Even though you and John Lennon played Śrīla Prabhupāda's record a lot and had chanted quite a bit on your own, you'd never really met any of the devotees. Yet when Gurudāsa, Śyāmasundara, and I [three of the six devotees sent from America to open the first Hare Kṛṣṇa temple in London] first came to England, you co-signed the lease on our first temple in central London, bought Bhaktivedanta Manor for us, which has provided a place

for literally hundreds of thousands of people to learn about Kṛṣṇa consciousness, and financed the first printing of the book *Kṛṣṇa*. You hadn't really known us for a very long time at all. Wasn't this a kind of sudden change for you?

George: Not really, for I always felt at home with Kṛṣṇa. You see, it was already a part of me. I think it's something that's been with me from my previous birth. Your coming to England and all that was just like another piece of a jigsaw puzzle that was coming together to make a complete picture. It had been slowly fitting together. That's why I responded to you all the way I did when you first came to London. Let's face it. If you're going to have to stand up and be counted, I figured, "I would rather be with these guys than with those other guys over there." It's like that. I mean I'd rather be one of the devotees of God than one of the straight, so-called sane or normal people who just don't understand that man is a spiritual being, that he has a soul. And I felt comfortable with you all, too – kind of like we'd known each other before. It was a pretty natural thing, really.

Mukunda: You were a member of the Beatles, undoubtedly the greatest single pop group in music history – one that influenced not only music but whole generations of young people. After the dissolution of the group, you went on to emerge as a solo superstar with albums like *All Things Must Pass,* the country's top-selling album for seven weeks in a row, and its hit single "My Sweet Lord," which was number one in America for two months. That was followed by *Living in the Material World,* number one on Billboard for five weeks and a million-selling LP. One song on that album, "Give Me Love," was a smash hit for six straight weeks. The concert for Bangladesh with Ringo Starr, Eric Clapton, Bob Dylan, Leon Russell, and Billy Preston was a phenomenal success and, once the LP and concert film were released, would become the single most successful rock benefit project ever. So, you had material success. You'd been everywhere, done everything, yet at the same time you were on a spiritual quest. What was it that really got you started on your spiritual journey?

George: It wasn't until the experience of the sixties really hit. You know, having been successful and meeting everybody we thought worth meeting and finding out they weren't worth meeting, and having had more hit records than everybody else and having done it bigger than everybody else. It was like reaching the top of a wall and then looking over and seeing that there's so much more on the other side. So I felt it was part of my duty to say, "Oh, okay, maybe you are thinking this is all you need – to be rich and famous – but actually it isn't."

Mukunda: In your recently published autobiography, *I, Me, Mine,* you said your song "Awaiting on You All" is about *japa* yoga, or chanting mantras on beads. You explained that a mantra is "mystical energy encased in a sound structure," and that "each mantra contains within its vibrations a certain power." But of all mantras, you stated that "the *mahā-mantra*" [the Hare Kṛṣṇa mantra] has been prescribed as the easiest and surest way for attaining God realization in this present age. As a practitioner of *japa* yoga, what realizations have you experienced from chanting?

George: Prabhupāda told me once that we should just keep chanting all the time – or as much as possible. Once you do that, you realize the benefit. The response that comes from chanting is in the form of bliss, or spiritual happiness, which is a much higher taste than any happiness found here in the material world. That's why I say that the more you do it, the more you don't want to stop, because it feels so nice and peaceful.

Mukunda: What is it about the mantra that brings about this feeling of peace and happiness?

George: The word *Hare* is the word that calls upon the energy that's around the Lord. If you say the mantra enough, you build up an identification with God. God's all happiness, all bliss, and by chanting His names we connect with Him. So it's really a process of actually having a realization of God, which all becomes clear with the expanded state of consciousness that develops when you chant. Like I said in the introduction I wrote for Prabhupāda's *Kṛṣṇa* book some years ago, "If there's a God, I want to see Him. It's pointless to believe in something without proof, and Kṛṣṇa consciousness and meditation are methods where you can actually obtain God perception."

Mukunda: Is it an instantaneous process, or gradual?

George: You don't get it in five minutes. It's something that takes time, but it works because it's a direct process of attaining God and will help us to have pure consciousness and good perception that is above the normal, everyday state of consciousness.

Mukunda: How do you feel after chanting for a long time?

George: In the life I lead, I find that I sometimes have opportunities when I can really get going at it, and the more I do it, I find the harder it is to stop, and I don't want to lose the feeling it gives me.

For example, once I chanted the Hare Kṛṣṇa mantra nonstop all the way from France to Portugal. I drove for about twenty-three hours and chanted all the way. It gets you feeling a bit invincible. The funny thing was that I didn't even know where I was going. I mean, I had bought a map and I knew basically which way I was aiming, but I couldn't speak French, Spanish, or Portuguese. But none of that seemed to matter. You know, once you get chanting, then things start to happen transcendentally.

Mukunda: The *Vedas* inform us that because God is absolute, there is no difference between God the person and His holy name; the name is God. When you first started chanting, could you perceive that?

George: It takes a certain amount of time and faith to accept or realize that there's no difference between Him and His name – to get to the point where you're no longer mystified by where He is. You know, like, "Is He around here?" You realize after some time, "Here He is – right here!" It's a matter of practice. So when I say that "I see God," I don't necessarily mean to say that when I chant I'm seeing Kṛṣṇa in His original form when He came five thousand years ago, dancing across the water, playing His flute. Of course, that would also be nice, and it's quite possible too. When you become real pure by chanting, you can actually see God like that – I mean personally. But no doubt you can feel His presence and know that He's there when you're chanting.

Mukunda: Can you think of any incident where you felt God's presence very strongly through chanting?

George: Once I was on an airplane that was in an electric storm. It was hit by lightning three times, and a Boeing 707 went over the top of us, missing us by inches. I thought the back end of the plane had blown off. I was on my way from Los Angeles to New York to organize the Bangladesh concert. As soon as the plane began bouncing around, I started chanting Hare Kṛṣṇa, Hare Kṛṣṇa, Kṛṣṇa Kṛṣṇa, Hare Hare/ Hare Rāma, Hare Rāma, Rāma Rāma, Hare Hare. The whole thing went on for about an hour and a half or two hours, the plane dropping hundreds of feet and bouncing all over in the storm, all the lights out and all these explosions, and everybody terrified. I ended up with my feet pressed against the seat in front, my seat belt as tight as it could be, gripping on the thing, and yelling Hare Kṛṣṇa, Hare Kṛṣṇa, Kṛṣṇa Kṛṣṇa, Hare Hare at the top of my voice. I know for me, the difference between making it and not making it was actually chanting the mantra. Peter Sellers also swore that chanting Hare Kṛṣṇa saved him from a plane crash once.

John Lennon and Hare Kṛṣṇa

Mukunda: Did any of the other Beatles chant?

George: Before meeting Prabhupāda and all of you I had

bought that album Prabhupāda did in New York, and John and I listened to it. I remember we sang it for days, John and I, with ukulele banjos, sailing through the Greek islands chanting Hare Kṛṣṇa. Like six hours we sang, because we couldn't stop once we got going. As soon as we stopped it was like the lights went out. It went on to the point where our jaws were aching, singing the mantra over and over and over and over and over. We felt exalted; it was a very happy time for us.

Mukunda: You know, I saw a video the other day sent to us from Canada, showing John and Yoko Ono recording their hit song "Give Peace a Chance," and about five or six of the devotees were there in John's room at the Queen Elizabeth Hotel in Montreal, singing along and playing cymbals and drums. You know, John and Yoko chanted Hare Kṛṣṇa on that song. That was in May of '69, and just three months later, Śrīla Prabhupāda was John and Yoko's houseguest for one month at their estate outside London.

While Prabhupāda was there, you, John, and Yoko came to his room one afternoon for a few hours. I think that was the first time you all met him.

George: That's right.

Mukunda: At that point John was a spiritual seeker, and Prabhupāda explained the true path to peace and liberation. He talked about karma, reincarnation, and the eternality of the soul, which are all elaborately dealt with in the Vedic literatures. Although John never made Hare Kṛṣṇa a big part of his life, he echoed the philosophy of Kṛṣṇa consciousness in a hit song he wrote just about a year after that conversation, "Instant Karma."

Now what's the difference between chanting Hare Kṛṣṇa and meditation?

George: It's really the same sort of thing as meditation, but I think it has a quicker effect. I mean, even if you put your beads down, you can still say the mantra or sing it without actually keeping track on your beads. One of the main differences between silent meditation and chanting is that silent meditation is rather dependent on concentration, but when you chant, it's more of a direct connection with God.

Practical Meditation

Mukunda: The *mahā-mantra* was prescribed for modern times because of the fast-paced nature of things today. Even when people do get into a little quiet place, it's very difficult to calm the mind for very long.

George: That's right. Chanting Hare Kṛṣṇa is a type of meditation that can be practiced even if the mind is in turbulence. You can even be doing it and other things at the same time. That's what's so nice. In my life there's been many times the mantra brought things around. It keeps me in tune with reality, and the more you sit in one place and chant, the more incense you offer to Kṛṣṇa in the same room, the more you purify the vibration, the more you can achieve what you're trying to do, which is just trying to remember God, God, God, God, God as often as possible. And if you're talking to Him with the mantra, it certainly helps.

Mukunda: What else helps you to fix your mind on God?

George: Well, just having as many things around me that will remind me of Him, like incense and pictures. Just the other day I was looking at a small picture on the wall of my studio of you, Gurudāsa, and Śyāmasundara, and just seeing all the old devotees made me think of Kṛṣṇa. I guess that's the business of devotees – to make you think of God.

Mukunda: How often do you chant?

George: Whenever I get a chance.

Mukunda: Once you asked Śrīla Prabhupāda about a particular verse he quoted from the *Vedas,* in which it's said that when one chants the holy name of Kṛṣṇa, Kṛṣṇa dances on the tongue and one wishes one had thousands of ears and thousands of mouths with which to better appreciate the holy names of God.

George: Yes. I think he was talking about the realization that there is no difference between Him standing before you and His being present in His name. That's the real beauty of chanting – you directly connect with God. I have no doubt that by saying Kṛṣṇa over and over again He can come and dance on the tongue. The main thing, though, is to keep in touch with God.

Mukunda: So your habit is generally to use the beads when you chant?

George: Oh, yeah. I have my beads. I remember when I first got them, they were just big knobby globs of wood, but now I'm very glad to say that they're smooth from chanting a lot.

Mukunda: Do you generally keep them in the bag when you chant?

George: Yes. I find it's very good to be touching them. It keeps another one of the senses fixed on God. Beads really help in that respect. You know, the frustrating thing about it was in the beginning there was a period when I was heavy into chanting and I had my hand in my bead bag all the time. And I got so tired of people asking me, "Did you hurt your hand – break it or something?" In the end I used to say, "Yeah, yeah. I had an accident," because it was easier than explaining everything. Using the beads also helps me to release a lot of nervous energy.

Mukunda: Some people say that if everyone on the planet chanted Hare Kṛṣṇa, they wouldn't be able to keep their minds on what they were doing. In other words, some people ask that if everyone started chanting, wouldn't the whole world just grind to a halt? They wonder if people would stop working in factories, for example.

George: No. Chanting doesn't stop you from being creative or productive. It actually helps you concentrate. I think this would make a great sketch for television: imagine all the workers on the Ford assembly line in Detroit, all of them chanting Hare Kṛṣṇa, Hare Kṛṣṇa while bolting on the wheels. Now that would be wonderful. It might help out the auto industry, and probably there would be more decent cars too.

Experiencing God Through the Senses

Mukunda: We've talked a lot about *japa,* or personalized chanting, which most chanters engage in. But there's another type, called *kīrtana,* when one chants congregationally, in a temple or on the street with a group of devotees. *Kīrtana* generally gives a more supercharged effect, like recharging one's spiritual batteries, and it gives others a chance to hear the holy names and become purified.

Actually, I was with Śrīla Prabhupāda when he first began the group chanting in Tompkins Square Park on New York's Lower East Side in 1966. The poet Allen Ginsberg would come and chant with us a lot and would play his harmonium. A lot of people would come to hear the chanting. Then Prabhupāda would give lectures on the *Bhagavad-gītā* back at the temple.

George: Yes, going to a temple or chanting with a group of other people – the vibration is that much stronger. Of course, for some people it's easy just to start chanting on their beads in the middle of a crowd, while other people are more comfortable chanting in the temple. But part of Kṛṣṇa consciousness is trying to tune in all the senses of all the people: to experience God through all the senses – not just by experiencing Him on Sunday, through your knees by kneeling on some hard wooden kneeler in the church. But if you visit a temple, you can see pictures of God, you can see the Deity form of the Lord, and you can just hear Him by listening to yourself and others say the mantra. It's just a way of realizing that all the senses can be applied to perceiving God, and it makes it that much more appealing, seeing the pictures, hearing the mantra, smelling the incense, flowers, and so on. That's the nice thing about your movement. It incorporates everything – chanting, dancing, philosophy, and *prasāda* [vegetarian food that has been spiritualized by being offered to Lord Kṛṣṇa]. The music and dancing is a serious part of the process too. It's not just something to burn off excess energy.

Mukunda: We've always seen that when we chant in the streets, people are eager to crowd around and listen. A lot of them tap their feet or dance along.

George: It's great – the sound of the cymbals. When I hear them from a few blocks away, it's like some magical thing that awakens something in me. Without their really being aware of what's happening, people are being awakened spiritually. Of course, in another sense, in a higher sense, the *kīrtana* is always going on whether we're hearing it or not.

Now, all over the place in Western cities, the *saṅkīrtana* party has become a common sight. I love to see these *saṅkīrtana* parties, because I love the whole idea of the devotees mixing it up with everybody – giving everybody a chance to remember. I wrote in the *Kṛṣṇa* book introduction, "Everybody is looking for Kṛṣṇa. Some don't realize that they are, but they are. Kṛṣṇa is God ... and by chanting His holy names, the devotee quickly develops God consciousness."

Mukunda: You know, Śrīla Prabhupāda often said that after a large number of temples were established most people would simply begin to take up the chanting of Hare Kṛṣṇa in their own homes, and we're seeing more and more that this is what's happening. Our worldwide congregation is very large – in the millions. The chanting on the streets, the books, and the temples are there to give people a start, to introduce them to the process.

George: I think it's better that it is spreading into the homes now. There are a lot of "closet Krishnas," you know.

There's a lot of people out there who are just waiting, and if it's not today it will be tomorrow or next week or next year.

Back in the sixties, whatever we were all getting into, we tended to broadcast it as loud as we could. I had certain realizations and went through a period where I was so thrilled about my discoveries and realizations that I wanted to shout and tell it to everybody. But there's a time to shout it out and a time not to shout it out. A lot of people went underground with their spiritual life in the seventies, but they're out there in little nooks and crannies and in the countryside, people who look and dress straight – insurance salesmen types – but they're really meditators and chanters – closet devotees.

Prabhupāda's movement is doing pretty well. It's growing like wildfire, really. How long it will take until we get to a golden age where everybody's perfectly in tune with God's will I don't know, but because of Prabhupāda, Kṛṣṇa consciousness has certainly spread more in the last sixteen years than it has since the sixteenth century, the time of Lord Caitanya.* The mantra has spread more quickly, and the movement's gotten bigger and bigger. It would be great if everyone chanted. Everybody would benefit by doing it. No matter how much money you've got, it doesn't necessarily make you happy. You have to find your happiness with the problems you have – not worry too much about them – and chant Hare Kṛṣṇa, Hare Kṛṣṇa, Kṛṣṇa Kṛṣṇa, Hare Hare.

The Hare Kṛṣṇa Record

Mukunda: In 1969 you produced a single called "The Hare Krishna Mantra," which eventually became a hit in many

* The great saint, mystic, and incarnation of Kṛṣṇa who popularized the chanting of Hare Kṛṣṇa and founded the modern-day Hare Kṛṣṇa movement.

countries. That tune later became a cut on the *Rādhā-Kṛṣṇa Temple* album, which you also produced on the Apple label and which was distributed in America by Capitol Records. A lot of people in the recording business were surprised by this – your producing songs for and singing with the Hare Kṛṣṇas. Why did you do it?

George: Well, it's just all a part of service, isn't it? Spiritual service – in order to try to spread the mantra all over the world. Also, to try and give the devotees a wider base and a bigger foothold in England and everywhere else.

Mukunda: How did the success of this record of Hare Kṛṣṇa devotees chanting compare with some of the rock musicians you were producing at the time like Jackie Lomax, Splinter, and Billy Preston?

George: It was a different thing. Nothing to do with that really. There was much more reason to do it. There was less commercial potential in it, but it was much more satisfying to do, knowing the possibilities that it was going to create, the connotations it would have just by doing a three-and-a-half-minute mantra. That was more fun really than trying to make a pop hit record. It was the feeling of trying to utilize your skills or job to make it into some spiritual service to Kṛṣṇa.

Mukunda: What effect do you think that tune, "The Hare Krishna Mantra," having reached millions and millions of people, has had on the world's cosmic consciousness?

George: I'd like to think it had some effect. After all, the sound is God.

Mukunda: When Apple called a press conference to promote the record, the media seemed shocked to hear you speak about the soul and God being so important.

George: I felt it was important to try and be precise – to tell them and let them know. You know, to come out of the closet and really tell them. Because once you realize something, then you can't pretend you don't know it anymore.

I figured this is the space age, with airplanes and everything. If everyone can go around the world on their holidays, there's no reason why a mantra can't go a few miles as well. So the idea was to try to spiritually infiltrate society, so to speak. After I got Apple Records committed to you and the record released, and after our big promotion, we saw it was going to become a hit. And one of the greatest things, one of the greatest thrills of my life, actually, was seeing you all on BBC's *Top of the Pops.* I couldn't believe it. It's pretty hard to get on that program, because they only put you on if you come into the top twenty. It was just like a breath of fresh air. My strategy was to keep it to a three-and-a-half-minute version of the mantra so they'd play it on the radio, and it worked. I did the harmonium and guitar track for that record at Abbey Road studios before one of the Beatles' sessions, and then overdubbed a bass part. I remember Paul McCartney and his wife, Linda, arrived at the studio and enjoyed the mantra.

Mukunda: Paul's quite favorable now, you know.

George: That's good. It still sounds like quite a good recording, even after all these years. It was the greatest fun of all, really, to see Kṛṣṇa on *Top of the Pops.*

Mukunda: Shortly after its release, John Lennon told me that they played it at the intermission right before Bob Dylan did the Isle of Wight concert with Jimi Hendrix, the Moody Blues, and Joe Cocker in the summer of '69.

George: They played it while they were getting the stage set up for Bob. It was great. Besides, it was a catchy tune, and the people didn't have to know what it meant in order to enjoy it. I felt very good when I first heard it was doing well.

Mukunda: How did you feel about the record technically – the voices?

George: Yamuna, the lead singer, has a naturally good voice. I liked the way she sang with conviction, and she sang like she'd been singing it a lot before. It didn't sound like the first tune she'd ever sung.

You know, I used to sing the mantra long before I met any of the devotees or long before I met Prabhupāda, because I had his first record then for at least two years. When you're open to something it's like being a beacon, and you attract it. From the first time I heard the chanting, it was like a door opened somewhere in my subconscious, maybe from some previous life.

Mukunda: In the lyrics to the song "Awaiting On You All" from *All Things Must Pass,* you come right out front and tell people that they can be free from living in the material world by chanting the names of God. What made you do it? What kind of feedback did you get?

George: At that time nobody was committed to that type of music in the pop world. There was, I felt, a real need for that, so rather than sitting and waiting for somebody else, I decided to do it myself. A lot of times we think, "Well, I agree with you, but I'm not going to actually stand up and be counted. Too risky." Everybody is always trying to keep themselves covered – stay commercial – so I thought, just do it. Nobody else is, and I'm sick of all these young people just boogeying around, wasting their lives, you know. Also, I felt that there were a lot of people out there who would be reached.

I still get letters from people saying, "I have been in the Kṛṣṇa temple for three years, and I would have never known about Kṛṣṇa unless you recorded the *All Things Must Pass* album." So I know, by the Lord's grace, I am a small part in the cosmic play.

Mukunda: What about the other Beatles? What did they think about your taking up Kṛṣṇa consciousness? What was their reaction? You'd all been to India by then and were pretty much searching for something spiritual. Śyāmasundara said that once, when he had lunch with you and the other Beatles, they were all quite respectful.

George: Oh, yeah, well, if the Fab Four didn't get it – that is, if they couldn't deal with shaven-headed Hare Kṛṣṇas –

then there would have been no hope! [Laughter.] And the devotees just came to be associated with me, so people stopped thinking, "Hey, what's this?" You know, if somebody in orange with a shaved head would appear, they'd say, "Oh, yeah, they're with George."

Mukunda: From the very start you always felt comfortable around the devotees?

George: The first time I met Śyāmasundara I liked him. He was my pal. On the back of Prabhupāda's record I'd read about Prabhupāda coming from India to Boston, and I knew that Śyāmasundara and all of you were in my age group, and that the only difference, really, was that you'd already joined and I hadn't. I was in a rock band, but I didn't have any fear, because I had seen *dhotīs* – your robes – and the saffron color and shaved heads in India. Kṛṣṇa consciousness was especially good for me because I didn't get the feeling that I'd have to shave my head, move into a temple, and do it full time. So it was a spiritual thing that just fit in with my lifestyle. I could still be a musician, but I just changed my consciousness, that's all.

Mukunda: You know, the Tudor mansion and estate that you gave us outside London has become one of our largest international centers. How do you feel about the Bhaktivedanta Manor's success in spreading Kṛṣṇa consciousness?

George: Oh, it's great. And it also relates to making the Hare Kṛṣṇa record or whatever my involvements were. Actually, it gives me pleasure – the idea that I was fortunate enough to be able to help at that time. All those songs with spiritual themes were like little plugs – "My Sweet Lord" and the others. And now I know that people are much more respectful and accepting when it comes to seeing the devotees in the streets and all that. It's no longer like something that's coming from left field.

And I've given a lot of Prabhupāda's books to many people, and whether I ever hear from them again or not, it's good to know that they've gotten them, and if they read them, their lives may be changed.

Mukunda: When you come across people who are spiritually inclined but don't have much knowledge, what kind of advice do you give them?

George: I try to tell them my little bit, what my experience is, and give them a choice of things to read and a choice of places to go – like you know, "Go to the temple, try chanting."

Mukunda: In the "Ballad of John and Yoko," John and Yoko rapped the media for the way it can foster a false image of you and perpetuate it. It's taken a lot of time and effort to get them to understand that we are a genuine religion, with scriptures that predate the New Testament by three thousand years. Gradually, though, more people – scholars, philosophers, theologians – have come around, and today they have a great deal of respect for the ancient Vaiṣṇava tradition [the spiritual culture centered on loving devotional service to Lord Viṣṇu, or Kṛṣṇa, the Supreme Personality of Godhead], where the modern-day Kṛṣṇa consciousness movement has its roots.

George: The media is to blame for *everything* – for all the misconceptions about the movement – but in a sense it didn't really matter if they said something good or bad, because Kṛṣṇa consciousness always seemed to transcend that barrier anyway. The fact that the media was letting people know about Kṛṣṇa was good in itself.

Mukunda: Śrīla Prabhupāda always trained us to stick to our principles. He said that the worst thing we could ever do would be to make some sort of compromise or to dilute the philosophy for the sake of cheap popularity. Although many swamis and yogis had come from India to the West, Prabhupāda was the only one with the purity and devotion to establish India's ancient Kṛṣṇa conscious philosophy around the world on its own terms – not watered down but as it is.

George: That's right. He was a perfect example of what he preached.

Mukunda: How did you feel about financing the first printing of the *Kṛṣṇa* book and writing the introduction?

George: I just felt like it was part of my job, you know. Wherever I go in the world, when I see devotees, I always say "Hare Kṛṣṇa!" to them, and they're always pleased to see me. It's a nice relationship. Whether they really know me personally or not, they feel they know me. And they do, really.

Mukunda: When you did the *Material World* album you used a photo insert taken from the cover of Prabhupāda's *Bhagavad-gītā* showing Kṛṣṇa and His friend and disciple Arjuna. Why?

George: Oh, yeah. It said on the album, "From the cover of *Bhagavad-gītā As It Is* by A. C. Bhaktivedanta Swami." It was a promo for you, of course. I wanted to give them all a chance to see Kṛṣṇa, to know about Him. I mean that's the whole idea, isn't it?

Spiritual Food

Mukunda: At lunch today we spoke a little about *prasāda,* vegetarian food that has been spiritualized by being offered to Kṛṣṇa in the temple. A lot of people have come to Kṛṣṇa consciousness through *prasāda,* especially through our Sunday Feast at all our centers around the world. I mean, this process is the only kind of yoga that you can actually practice by eating.

George: Well, we should try to see God in everything, so it helps so much having the food to taste. Let's face it, if God is in everything, why shouldn't you taste Him when you eat? I think that *prasāda* is a very important thing. Kṛṣṇa is God, so He's absolute: His name, His form, *prasāda* – it's all Him. They say the way to a man's heart is through his stomach, so if you can get to a man's spirit soul by eating, and it works, why not do it? There's nothing better than having been chanting and dancing, or just sitting and talking philosophy, and then suddenly the devotees bring out the *prasāda*. It's a blessing from Kṛṣṇa, and it's spiritually important.

The idea is that *prasāda* is the sacrament the Christians talk about, only instead of being just a wafer, it's a whole feast, really, and the taste is so nice – it's out of this world. And *prasāda's* a good little hook in this age of commercialism. When people want something extra, or they need to have something special, *prasāda* will hook them in there. It's undoubtedly done a great deal toward getting a lot more people involved in spiritual life. It breaks down prejudices, too. Because they think, "Oh, well, yes, I wouldn't mind a drink of whatever or a bite of that." Then they ask, "What's this?" and "Oh, well, it's *prasāda*." And they get to learn another aspect of Kṛṣṇa consciousness. Then they say, "It actually tastes quite nice. Have you got another plateful?" I've seen that happen with lots of people, especially older people I've seen at your temples. Maybe they were a little prejudiced, but the next thing you know, they're in love with *prasāda,* and eventually they walk out of the temple thinking, "They're not so bad after all."

Mukunda: The Vedic literatures reveal that *prasāda* conveys spiritual realization, just as chanting does, but in a less obvious or conspicuous way. You make spiritual advancement just by eating it.

George: I'd say from my experience that it definitely works. I've always enjoyed *prasāda* much more when I've been at the temple, or when I've actually been sitting with Prabhupāda, than when somebody's brought it to me. Sometimes you can sit there with *prasāda* and find that three or four hours have gone by and you didn't even know it. *Prasāda* really helped me a lot, because you start to realize, "Now I'm tasting Kṛṣṇa." You're conscious suddenly of another aspect of God, understanding that He's this little *samosā*. It's all just a matter of tuning into the spiritual, and *prasāda's* a very real part of it all.

Mukunda: You know, a lot of the rock groups like the Grateful Dead and Police get *prasāda* backstage before their concerts. They love it. It's a long-standing tradition with us. I remember one time sending *prasāda* to one of the Beatles' recording sessions. And your sister was telling me today that while you were doing the Bangladesh concert, Śyāmasundara used to bring you all *prasāda* at the rehearsals.

George: Yes, he's even got a credit on the album sleeve.

Mukunda: What are your favorite kinds of *prasāda*, George?

George: I really like those deep-fried cauliflower things – *pakorās*?

Mukunda: Yes.

George: And one thing I always liked was *ras malai*. And there're a lot of good drinks as well – fruit juices and *lassi*.

Mukunda: Do you remember the time we called the press in London for a big feast when we were promoting "The Hare Krishna Mantra" record? They were pretty surprised, for no one really knew us then for our food. Now, pretty much when people think about us, they still think, "They're the ones chanting and dancing in the streets," but they're connecting us more and more now with *prasāda:* "They're the ones with those free vegetarian dinners."

George: The press was probably thinking, "Oh, we've got to go and do this now." And then suddenly they find that they're all sitting around and eating a much better Indian take-away than they would ever have at any one of the local spots. They were pretty impressed.

Mukunda: We've served about 150 million plates of *prasāda* so far at the free feasts around the world, what to speak of our restaurants.

George: You ought to have it up outside on billboards like those hamburger places do. You know, like "150 million served." I think it's great. It's a pity you don't have restaurants or temples on all the main streets of every little town and village like those hamburger and fried chicken places. You should put them out of business.

Mukunda: You've been to our London restaurant, Healthy, Wealthy, and Wise?

George: Lots of times. It's good to have these and other restaurants around, where plainclothes devotees serve the food. People slowly realize, "This is one of the best places I've been," and they keep coming back. Then maybe they pick up a little bit of the literature or a pamphlet there and say, "Oh, hey, that was run by the Hare Kṛṣṇas." I think there's a lot of value also to that kind of more subtle approach. Healthy, Wealthy, and Wise has proper foods, good, balanced stuff, and it's fresh. Even more important, it's made with an attitude of devotion, which means a lot. When you know someone has begrudgingly cooked something, it doesn't taste as nice as when someone has done it to try and please God – to offer it to Him first. Just that in itself makes all the food taste so much nicer.

Mukunda: Paul and Linda McCartney have *prasāda* frequently from Healthy, Wealthy, and Wise. Not long ago Paul met a devotee near his London studio and wrote a song about it. In an interview with James Johnson in a London paper he said, "One song, 'One of These Days,' is about when I met someone on the way to the studio who was a Hare Kṛṣṇa and we got talking about lifestyles and so forth. I'm not a Hare Kṛṣṇa myself, but I'm very sympathetic."

You've been a vegetarian for years, George. Have you had any difficulties maintaining it?

George: No. Actually, I wised up and made sure I had *dāl* bean soup or something every day. Actually, lentils are one of the cheapest things, but they give you A1 protein. People are simply screwing up when they go out and buy beef steak, which is killing them with cancer and heart troubles. The stuff costs a fortune too. You could feed a thousand people with lentil soup for the cost of half a dozen fillets. Does that make sense?

Mukunda: One of the things that really has a profound effect on people when they visit the temples or read our books is the paintings and sculptures done by our devotee artists of scenes from Kṛṣṇa's pastimes when He appeared on earth five thousand years ago. Prabhupāda once said that these paintings were "windows to the spiritual world," and he organized an art academy, training his disciples in the techniques for creating transcendental art. Now, tens of thousands of people have these paintings hanging in their homes, either as originals, lithographs, canvas prints, or posters. You've been to our multimedia *Bhagavad-gītā* museum in Los Angeles. What kind of an effect did it have on you?

George: I thought it was great – better than Disneyland, really. I mean, it's as valuable as that, or the Smithsonian Institute in Washington. The sculpted dioramas look great, and the music is nice. It gives people a real feeling for what the kingdom of God must be like, and much more basic than that, it shows in a way that's easy for even a child to understand exactly how the body is different from the soul and how the soul's the important thing. I always have pictures around like the one of Kṛṣṇa on the chariot that I put in the *Material World* album, and I have the sculpted Śiva fountain* the devotees made for me in my garden. Pictures are helpful when I'm chanting. You know that painting in the *Bhagavad-gītā* of the Supersoul in the heart of the dog, the cow, the elephant, the poor man, and the priest? That's very good to help you realize that Kṛṣṇa is dwelling

* After seeing the dioramas at the Los Angeles *Bhagavad-gītā* museum, George asked if the artists and sculptors who had produced the museum could sculpt a life-sized fountain of Lord Śiva, one of the principal Hindu demigods and a great devotee of Lord Kṛṣṇa. Lord Śiva, in a meditative pose, complete with a stream of water spouting from his head, soon resided in the gardens of George's estate, heralded as among the most beautiful in all of England.

in the hearts of everybody. It doesn't matter what kind of body you've got – the Lord's there with you. We're all the same, really.

Meeting Śrīla Prabhupāda

Mukunda: George, you and John Lennon met Śrīla Prabhupāda together when he stayed at John's home in September of 1969.
George: Yes, but when I met him at first, I underestimated him. I didn't realize it then, but I see now that because of him, the mantra has spread so far in the last sixteen years – more than it had in the last five centuries. Now that's pretty amazing, because he was getting older and older, yet he was writing his books all the time. I realized later on that he was much more incredible than what you could see on the surface.
Mukunda: What about him stands out the most in your mind?
George: The thing that always stays is his saying "I am the servant of the servant of the servant." I like that. A lot of people say "I'm it. I'm the divine incarnation. I'm here and let me hip you." You know what I mean? But Prabhupāda was never like that. I liked Prabhupāda's humbleness. I always liked his humility and his simplicity. The servant of the servant of the servant is really what it is, you know. None of us are God – just His servants. He just made me feel so comfortable. I always felt very relaxed with him, and I felt more like a friend. I felt that he was a good friend. Even though he was at the time seventy-three years old, working practically all through the night, day after day, with very little sleep, he still didn't come through to me as though he was a very highly educated intellectual being, because he had a sort of childlike simplicity. Which is great – fantastic. Even though he was the greatest Sanskrit scholar and a saint, I appreciated the fact that he never made me feel

uncomfortable. In fact, he always went out of his way to make me feel comfortable. I always thought of him as sort of a lovely friend, really, and now he's still a lovely friend.

Mukunda: In one of his books, Prabhupāda said that your sincere service was better than some people who had delved more deeply into Kṛṣṇa consciousness but could not maintain that level of commitment. How did you feel about that?

George: Very wonderful, really. I mean it really gave me hope, because as they say, even one moment in the company of a divine person – Kṛṣṇa's pure devotee – can help a tremendous amount.

And I think Prabhupāda was really pleased at the idea that somebody from outside the temple was helping to get the album made. Just the fact that he was pleased was encouraging to me. I knew he liked "The Hare Krishna Mantra" record, and he asked the devotees to play that song "Govinda." They still play it, don't they?

Mukunda: Every temple has a recording of it, and we play it each morning when the devotees assemble before the altar, before *kīrtana*. It's an ISKCON institution, you might say.

George: And if I didn't get feedback from Prabhupāda on my songs about Kṛṣṇa or the philosophy, I'd get it from the devotees. That's all the encouragement I needed, really. It just seemed that anything spiritual I did, either through songs or helping with publishing the books or whatever, really pleased him. My song "Living in the Material World," as I wrote in *I, Me, Mine,* was influenced by Śrīla Prabhupāda. He's the one who explained to me how we're not these physical bodies. We just happen to be *in* them.

Like I said in the song, this place's not really what's happening. We don't belong here but in the spiritual sky:

As I'm fated for the material world
Get frustrated in the material world

Senses never gratified
Only swelling like a tide
That could drown me in the material world

The whole point to being here, really, is to figure a way to get out.

That was the thing about Prabhupāda, you see. He didn't just talk about loving Kṛṣṇa and getting out of this place; he was the perfect example. He talked about always chanting, and he was always chanting. I think that that in itself was perhaps the most encouraging thing for me. It was enough to make me try harder, to be just a little bit better. He was a perfect example of everything he preached.

Mukunda: How would you describe Śrīla Prabhupāda's achievements?

George: I think Prabhupāda's accomplishments are very significant; they're huge. Even compared to someone like William Shakespeare, the amount of literature Prabhupāda produced is truly amazing. It boggles the mind. He sometimes went for days with only a few hours' sleep. I mean even a youthful, athletic young person couldn't keep the pace he kept up at seventy-nine years of age.

Śrīla Prabhupāda has already had an amazing effect on the world. There's no way of measuring it. One day I just realized, "God, this man is amazing!" He would sit up all night translating Sanskrit into English, putting in glossaries to make sure everyone understands it, and yet he never came off as someone above you. He always had that childlike simplicity. And what's most amazing is the fact that he did all this translating in such a relatively short time – just a few years. And without having anything more than his own Kṛṣṇa consciousness, he rounded up all these thousands of devotees, set the whole movement in motion, which became something so strong that it went on even after he passed away in 1977. And it's still escalating even now at an incredible rate. It will go on and on from the knowledge he gave. It can only grow and grow. The more people wake up spiritually, the more they'll begin to realize the depth of what Prabhupāda was saying – how much he gave.

Mukunda: Did you know that complete sets of Prabhupāda's books are in all the major colleges and universities in the world, including Harvard, Yale, Princeton, Oxford, Cambridge, and the Sorbonne?

George: They should be! One of the greatest things I noticed about Prabhupāda was the way he would be talking to you in English, and then all of a sudden he would say it to you in Sanskrit, and then translate it back into English. It was clear that he really knew it well. His contribution has obviously been enormous from the literary point of view because he's brought the Supreme Person, Kṛṣṇa, more into focus. A lot of scholars and writers know the *Gītā,* but only on an intellectual level. Even when they write "Kṛṣṇa said . . .," they don't do it with the *bhakti* or love required. That's the secret, you know – Kṛṣṇa is actually a person who is the Lord and who will also appear there in that book when there is that love, that *bhakti*. You can't understand the first thing about God unless you love Him. These big, so-called Vedic scholars – they don't necessarily love Kṛṣṇa, so they can't understand Him and give Him to us. But Prabhupāda was different.

Mukunda: The Vedic literatures predicted that after the advent of Lord Caitanya five hundred years ago there would be a golden age of ten thousand years, when the chanting of the holy names of God would completely nullify all the degradations of the modern age, and real spiritual peace would come to this planet.

George: Well, Prabhupāda's definitely affected the world in an absolute way. What he was giving us was the highest literature, the highest knowledge. I mean there just isn't anything higher.

Mukunda: You write in your autobiography that "No

matter how good you are, you still need grace to get out of the material world. You can be a yogi or a monk or a nun, but without God's grace you still can't make it." And at the end of the song "Living in the Material World," the lyrics say, "Got to get out of this place by the Lord Śrī Kṛṣṇa's grace, my salvation from the material world." If we're dependent on the grace of God, what does the expression "God helps those who help themselves" mean?

George: It's flexible, I think. In one way, I'm never going to get out of here unless it's by His grace, but then again, His grace is relative to the amount of desire I can manifest in myself. The amount of grace I would expect from God should be equal to the amount of grace I can gather or earn. I get out what I put in. Like in the song I wrote about Prabhupāda:

The Lord loves the one that loves the Lord
And the law says if you don't give
Then you don't get loving
Now the Lord helps those that help themselves
And the law says whatever you do
Is going to come right back on you

"The Lord Loves The One (That Loves The Lord)"
from *Living in the Material World*

Have you heard that song "That Which I Have Lost," from my new album, *Somewhere in England*? It's right out of the *Bhagavad-gītā*. In it I talk about fighting the forces of darkness, limitations, falsehood, and mortality.

God Is a Person

Mukunda: Yes, I like it. If people can understand the Lord's message in the *Bhagavad-gītā,* they can become truly happy. A lot of people, when they just get started in spiritual life, worship God as impersonal. What's the difference between worshiping Kṛṣṇa, or God, in His personal form and worshiping His impersonal nature as energy or light?

George: It's like the difference between hanging out with a computer or hanging out with a person. Like I said earlier, "If there is a God, I want to see Him," not only His energy or His light but Him.

Mukunda: What do you think is the goal of human life?

George: Each individual has to burn out his own karma and escape from the chains of *māyā* [illusory energy], reincarnation, and all that. The best thing anyone can give to humanity is God consciousness. Then you can really give them something. But first you have to concentrate on your own spiritual advancement. So in a sense we have to become selfish to become selfless.

Mukunda: What about trying to solve the problems of life without employing the spiritual process?

George: Life is like a piece of string with a lot of knots tied in it. The knots are the karma you're born with from all your past lives, and the object of human life is to try and undo all those knots. That's what chanting and meditation in God consciousness can do. Otherwise you simply tie another ten knots each time you try to undo one knot. That's how karma works. I mean, we're now the results of our past actions, and in the future we'll be the results of the actions we're performing now. A little understanding of "As you sow, so shall you reap" is important because then you can't blame the condition you're in on anyone else. You know that it's by your own actions you're able to get more in a mess or out of one. It's your own actions that relieve or bind you.

Mukunda: In the *Śrīmad-Bhāgavatam,* the crest jewel of all the Vedic literatures, it's described how those pure souls who live in the spiritual world with God have different types of *rasas,* or relationships, with Him. Is there any special way you like to think of Kṛṣṇa?

George: I like the idea of seeing Kṛṣṇa as a baby, the way He's often depicted in India. And also Govinda, the cowherd boy. I like the idea that you can have Kṛṣṇa as a baby and feel protective of Him, or as your friend, or as the guru or master-type figure.

"My Sweet Lord"

Mukunda: I don't think it's possible to calculate just how many people were turned on to Kṛṣṇa consciousness by your song "My Sweet Lord." But you went through quite a personal thing before you decided to do that song. In your book you write, "I thought a lot about whether to do 'My Sweet Lord' or not because I would be committing myself publicly ... Many people fear the words *Lord* and *God* ... I was sticking my neck out on the chopping block ... but at the same time I thought 'Nobody's saying it ... why should I be untrue to myself?' I came to believe in the importance that if you feel something strong enough, then you should say it.

"I wanted to show that Hallelujah and Hare Kṛṣṇa are quite the same thing. I did the voices singing 'Hallelujah' and then the change to 'Hare Kṛṣṇa' so that people would be chanting the *mahā-mantra* – before they knew what was going on! I had been chanting Hare Kṛṣṇa for a long time, and this song was a simple idea of how to do a Western pop equivalent of a mantra which repeats over and over again the holy names. I don't feel guilty or bad about it; in fact it saved many a heroin addict's life."

Why did you feel you wanted to put Hare Kṛṣṇa on the album at all? Wouldn't Hallelujah alone have been good enough?

George: Well, first of all Hallelujah is a joyous expression the Christians have, but Hare Kṛṣṇa has a mystical side to it. It's more than just glorifying God; it's asking to become His servant. And because of the way the mantra is put together, with the mystic spiritual energy contained in those syllables, it's much closer to God than the way Christianity currently seems to be representing Him. Although Christ in my mind is an absolute yogi, I think many Christian teachers today are misrepresenting Christ. They're supposed to be representing Jesus, but they're not doing it very well. They're letting him down very badly, and that's a big turn off.

My idea in "My Sweet Lord," because it sounded like a pop song, was to sneak up on them a bit. The point was to have the people not offended by Hallelujah, and by the time it gets to Hare Kṛṣṇa they're already hooked and their feet are tapping, and they're already singing Hallelujah – to kind of lull them into a sense of false security. And then suddenly it turns into Hare Kṛṣṇa, and they will all be singing that before they know what's happened, and they will think, "Hey, I thought I wasn't supposed to like Hare Kṛṣṇa!"

People write to me even now asking what style that was. Ten years later they're still trying to figure out what the words mean. It was just a little trick really. And it didn't offend. For some reason I never got any offensive feedback from Christians who said, "We like it up to a point, but what's all this about Hare Kṛṣṇa?"

Hallelujah may have originally been some mantric thing that got watered down, but I'm not sure what it really means. The Greek word for Christ is *Kristos,* which is, let's face it, Kṛṣṇa and *Kristos* is the same name actually.

Mukunda: What would you say is the difference between the Christian view of God and Kṛṣṇa as represented in the *Bhagavad-gītā*?

George: When I first came to this house it was occupied by nuns. I brought in this poster of Viṣṇu. You just see His head and shoulders and His four arms holding a conch shell and various other symbols, and it has a big *om* written above it. He has a nice aura around Him. I left it by the fireplace and went out into the garden. When we came back into the house, they all pounced on me, saying, "Who is that? What is it?" as if it were some pagan god. So I said, "Well, if God is unlimited, then He can appear in any form, whichever way He likes to appear. That's one way. He's called Viṣṇu."

It sort of freaked them out a bit, but the point is, why should God be limited? Even if you get Him as Kṛṣṇa, He is not limited to that picture of Kṛṣṇa. He can be the baby form, He can be Govinda, and He can manifest in so many other well-known forms. You can see Kṛṣṇa as a little boy, which is how I like to see Kṛṣṇa. It's a joyful relationship. But there's this morbid side to the way many represent Christianity today, where you don't smile, because it's too serious, and you can't expect to see God – that kind of stuff. If there is God, we must see Him, and I don't believe in the idea you find in most churches, where they say, "No, you're not going to see Him. He's way up above you. Just believe what we tell you and shut up."

I mean, the knowledge that's given in Prabhupāda's books – the Vedic stuff – that's the world's oldest scriptures. They say that man can become purified, and with divine vision he can see God. You get pure by chanting. Then you see Him. And Sanskrit, the language they're written in, is the world's first recorded language. Devanāgarī [the Sanskrit alphabets] actually means "language of the gods."

Mukunda: Anyone who is sincere about making spiritual advancement, whatever one's religion may be, can usually see the value of chanting – I mean, if that person is really trying to be God conscious and trying to chant sincerely.

George: That's right. It's a matter of being open. Anyone who's open can do it. You just have to be open and not prejudiced. You just have to try it. There's no loss, you know. But the "intellectuals" will always have problems, because they always need to "know." They're often the most spiritually bankrupt people because they never let go; they don't understand the meaning of "to transcend the intellect." But an ordinary person's more willing to say, "Okay, let me try it and see if it works." Chanting Hare Kṛṣṇa can make a person a better Christian, too.

Karma and Reincarnation

Mukunda: In *I, Me, Mine* you speak about karma and reincarnation, and how the only way to get out of the cycle is to take up a bona fide spiritual process. You say at one point, "Everybody is worried about dying, but the cause of death is birth, so if you don't want to die, you don't get born!" Did any of the other Beatles believe in reincarnation?

George: I'm sure John does! And I wouldn't want to underestimate Paul and Ringo. I wouldn't be surprised if they're hoping it's true, you know what I mean? For all I know, Ringo might be a yogi disguised as a drummer!

Mukunda: Paul had our latest book *Coming Back: The Science of Reincarnation.* Where do you think John's soul is now?

George: I should hope that he's in a good place. He had the understanding, though, that each soul reincarnates until it becomes completely pure, and that each soul finds its own level, designated by reactions to its actions in this and previous lives.

Mukunda: Bob Dylan did a lot of chanting at one time. He used to come to the Los Angeles temple and came to the Denver and Chicago temples as well. In fact, he drove across the United States with two devotees once and wrote several songs about Kṛṣṇa. They spent a lot of time chanting.

George: That's right. He said he enjoyed the chanting and being with them. Also, Stevie Wonder had you on one of his records, you know. And it was great – the song he put the chanting in, "Pastimes Paradise."

Mukunda: When you were in Vṛndāvana, India, where Lord Kṛṣṇa appeared, and you saw thousands of people chanting Hare Kṛṣṇa, did it strengthen your faith in the idea of chanting to see a whole city living Hare Kṛṣṇa?

George: Yeah, it fortifies you. It definitely helps. It's fantastic to be in a place where the whole town is doing it. And I also had the idea that they were all knocked out at the idea of seeing some white person chanting on beads. Vṛndāvana is one of the holiest cities in India. Everyone, everywhere, chants Hare Kṛṣṇa. It was my most fantastic experience.

Mukunda: You write in your book: "Most of the world is fooling about, especially the people who think they control the world and the community. The presidents, the politicians, the military, etc., are all jerking about, acting as if they are Lord over their own domains. That's basically Problem One on the planet."

George: That's right. Unless you're doing some kind of God conscious thing and you know that He's the one who's really in charge, you're just building up a lot of karma and not really helping yourself or anybody else. There's a point in me where it's beyond sad, seeing the state of the world today. It's so screwed up. It's terrible, and it will be getting worse and worse. More concrete everywhere, more pollution, more radioactivity. There's no wilderness left, no pure air. They're chopping the forests down. They're polluting all the oceans. In one sense, I'm pessimistic about the future of the planet. These big guys don't realize for everything they do there's a reaction. You have to pay. That's karma.

Mukunda: Do you think there's any hope?

George: Yes. One by one, everybody's got to escape *māyā*. Everybody has to burn out his karma and escape reincarnation and all that. Stop thinking that if Britain or America or Russia or the West or whatever becomes superior, then we'll beat them, and then we'll all have a rest and live happily ever after. That doesn't work. The best thing you can give is God consciousness. Manifest your own divinity first. The truth is there. It's right within us all. Understand what you are. If people would just wake up to what's real, there would be no misery in the world. I guess chanting's a pretty good place to start.

Mukunda: Thanks so much, George.

George: All right. Hare Kṛṣṇa!

CHAPTER TWO

Chanting for Liberation

A conversation about the Hare Kṛṣṇa mantra between Śrīla Prabhupāda and John Lennon, Yoko Ono, and George Harrison

Montreal Star, June 1969:

Reporter: Where do you get your strength?
John Lennon: From Hare Kṛṣṇa.
Yoko: That's where we get it from, you know. We're not denying it.

*In September 1969, A. C. Bhaktivedanta Swami Prabhupāda, founder-*ācārya *of the Hare Kṛṣṇa movement, arrived as a houseguest at Tittenhurst Park, the beautiful 72-acre British estate once owned by John Lennon and later by Ringo Starr. Three or four times a week, the Swami, who later became known to the world as Śrīla Prabhupāda, gave public lectures in a tall, stately building at the northern end of the property a hundred yards from the main house, in which John and Yoko lived.*

The building had formerly been used as a hall for chamber music recitals, but now several of Śrīla Prabhupāda's disciples, who resided along with him in a block of guesthouses on the property, installed a small Deity altar and a podium for Śrīla Prabhupāda. The building never really had a name, but after Śrīla Prabhupāda's arrival, everyone called it "The Temple."

On September 14, 1969 John, Yoko, and George Harrison, after enjoying an Indian vegetarian meal prepared by the devotees at The Temple, walked over to Śrīla Prabhupāda's quarters for their first meeting.

Which Mantra to Chant

Yoko Ono: If Hare Kṛṣṇa is such a strong, powerful mantra, is there any reason to chant anything else? For instance, you talked about songs and different mantras. Is there any point in chanting another song or mantra?

Śrīla Prabhupāda: There are other mantras, but the Hare Kṛṣṇa mantra is especially recommended for this age. But other Vedic mantras are also chanted. As I told you, the sages would sit with musical instruments, like the tamboura, and chant them. For instance, Narada Muni [a liberated sage who travels throughout the universe teaching love of God] is always chanting mantras and playing his stringed instrument, the *vīṇā*. So chanting out loud, with musical instruments, is not a new thing. It's been done since time immemorial. But the chanting of the Hare Kṛṣṇa mantra is especially recommended for this age. This is stated in many Vedic literatures, such as the *Brahmāṇḍa Purāṇa*, the *Kali-santaraṇa Upaniṣad*, the *Agni Purāṇa*, and so forth. And apart from the statements of the Vedic literature, Lord Kṛṣṇa Himself, in the form of Lord Caitanya, preached that everyone should chant the Hare Kṛṣṇa mantra. And many people followed Him. When a scientist discovers something, it becomes public property. People may take advantage of it. Similarly, if a mantra has potency, all people should be able to take advantage of it. Why should it remain secret? If a mantra is valuable, it is valuable for everybody. Why should it be for only a particular person?

John Lennon: If all mantras are just the name of God, then whether it's a secret mantra or an open mantra it's all the name of God. So it doesn't really make much difference, does it, which one you sing?

Śrīla Prabhupāda: It *does* make a difference. For instance, in a drug shop they sell all types of medicines for curing different diseases. But still you have to get a doctor's prescription in order to get a particular type of medicine. Otherwise, the druggist won't supply you. You might go to the drug shop and say, "I'm diseased. Please give me any medicine you have." But the druggist will ask you, "Where is your prescription?"

Prescription for the Age of Kali

Similarly, in this Age of Kali [the present age of quarrel and hypocrisy] the Hare Kṛṣṇa mantra is prescribed in the *śāstras,* or scriptures. And the great teacher Caitanya Mahāprabhu, whom we consider an incarnation of God, also prescribed it. Therefore, our principle is that everyone should follow the prescription of the great authorities, and we should follow in their footsteps. That is our business. As stated in the *Mahābhārata* (*Vana-pārva* 313.117):

tarko 'pratiṣṭhaḥ śrutayo vibhinnā
nāsāv ṛṣir yasya mataṁ na bhinnam
dharmasya tattvaṁ nihitaṁ guhāyāṁ
mahājano yena gataḥ sa panthāḥ

This Vedic mantra says that if you simply try to argue and approach the Absolute Truth, it is very difficult. By argument and reason it is very difficult, because our arguments and reason are limited. And our senses are imperfect. There are many confusing varieties of scriptures, and every philosopher has a different opinion, and unless a philosopher defeats other philosophers, he cannot become recognized as a big philosopher. One theory replaces another, and therefore philosophical speculation will not help us arrive at the Absolute Truth. The Absolute Truth is very secret. So how can one achieve such a secret thing? You simply follow the great personalities who have already achieved success. So our Kṛṣṇa consciousness philosophical method is to follow the great personalities, such as Lord Kṛṣṇa, Lord Caitanya, and the great spiritual masters in disciplic succession. Take shelter of bona fide authorities and follow them – that is recommended in the *Vedas*. That will take you to the ultimate goal.

You Can't Manufacture a Mantra

In the fourth chapter of the *Bhagavad-gītā* Śrī Kṛṣṇa says the same thing to Arjuna. *Evaṁ paramparā-prāptam:* In this way, by disciplic succession, the knowledge is coming down. *Sa kāleneha mahatā yogo naṣṭaḥ paran-tapa:* But in the course of time the succession was broken. Therefore, Kṛṣṇa says, "I am speaking it to you again." So a mantra should be received from the disciplic succession. The Vedic injunction is *sampradāya-vihinā ye mantrās te niṣphalā matāḥ*. If your mantra does not come through the disciplic succession, it will not be effective. *Mantrās te niṣphalā. Niṣphalā* means that it will not produce the desired result. So the mantra must be received through the proper channel, or it will not act. A mantra cannot be manufactured. It must originate with the Supreme Absolute and come down through the channel of disciplic succession. It has to be received in that way, and only then will it act.

According to our Kṛṣṇa consciousness philosophy, the mantra is coming down through four channels of disciplic succession: one through Lord Śiva, one through the goddess Lakṣmī, one through Lord Brahmā, and one through the four Kumāras. The same thing comes down through different channels. These are called the four *sampradāyas,* or disciplic successions. So, one has to take his mantra from one of these four *sampradāyas;* then only is that mantra active. If we receive the mantra in that way, it will be effective. And if one does not receive his mantra through one of these *sampradāya* channels, then it will not act; it will not give fruit.

Yoko Ono: If the mantra itself has such power, does it matter where you receive it, where you take it?

Śrīla Prabhupāda: Yes, it does matter. For instance, milk is nutritious. That's a fact; everyone knows. But if milk is touched by the lips of a serpent, it is no longer nutritious. It becomes poisonous.

Yoko Ono: Well, milk is material.

Śrīla Prabhupāda: Yes, it is material. But since you are trying to understand spiritual topics through your material senses, we have to give material examples.

Yoko Ono: Well, no, I don't think you have to give me the material sense. I mean, the mantra is not material. It should be something spiritual; therefore, I don't think anybody should be able to spoil it. I wonder if anybody can actually spoil something that isn't material.

Śrīla Prabhupāda: But if you don't receive the mantra through the proper channel, it may not really be spiritual.

John Lennon: How would you know, anyway? How are you able to tell? I mean, for any of your disciples or us or anybody else who goes to any spiritual master – how are we to tell if he's for real or not?

Śrīla Prabhupāda: You shouldn't go to just *any* spiritual master.

Who's a Genuine Guru?

John Lennon: Yes, we should go to a true master. But how are we to tell one from the other?
Śrīla Prabhupāda: It is not that you can go to just any spiritual master. He must be a member of a recognized *sampradāya,* a particular line of disciplic succession.
John Lennon: But what if one of these masters who's not in the line says exactly the same thing as one who is? What if he says his mantra is coming from the *Vedas* and he seems to speak with as much authority as you? He could probably be right. It's confusing – like having too many fruits on a plate.
Śrīla Prabhupāda: If the mantra is actually coming through a bona fide disciplic succession, then it will have potency.
John Lennon: But the Hare Kṛṣṇa mantra is the best one?
Śrīla Prabhupāda: Yes.
Yoko Ono: Well, if Hare Kṛṣṇa is the best one, why should we bother to say anything else other than Hare Kṛṣṇa?
Śrīla Prabhupāda: It's true: you don't have to bother with anything else. We say that the Hare Kṛṣṇa mantra is sufficient for one's perfection, for liberation.
George Harrison: Isn't it like flowers? Somebody may prefer roses, and somebody may like carnations better. Isn't it really a matter for the individual devotee to decide? One person may find that Hare Kṛṣṇa is more beneficial to his spiritual progress, and yet another person may find that some other mantra may be more beneficial for him. Isn't it just a matter of taste, like choosing a flower? They're all flowers, but some people may like one better than another.
Śrīla Prabhupāda: But still there is a distinction. A fragrant rose is considered better than a flower without any scent.

Yoko Ono: In that case, I can't . . .

Śrīla Prabhupāda: Let's try to understand this flower example.

Yoko Ono: Okay.

Śrīla Prabhupāda: You may be attracted by one flower and I may be attracted by another flower, but among the flowers a distinction can be made. There are many flowers that have no fragrance and many that have fragrance.

Yoko Ono: Is the flower that has fragrance better?

Śrīla Prabhupāda: Yes. Therefore, your attraction for a particular flower is not the solution to the question of which is actually better. In the same way, personal attraction is not the solution to choosing the best spiritual process. In the *Bhagavad-gītā,* Lord Kṛṣṇa says, "As all surrender to Me, I reward them accordingly. Everyone follows My path in all respects, O son of Pṛthā." Kṛṣṇa is the Supreme Absolute. If someone wants to enjoy a particular relationship with Him, Kṛṣṇa presents Himself in that way. It's just like the flower example. You may want a yellow flower, and that flower may not have any fragrance. That flower is there; it's for you – that's all. But if someone wants a rose, Kṛṣṇa gives him a rose. You both get the flower of your choice, but when you make a comparative study of which is better, the rose will be considered better.

Yoko Ono: I see a pattern in what you've said. For instance, you said that Hare Kṛṣṇa is the most super-powerful word. And if that is true, then why do we bother to utter any other words? I mean, is it necessary? And why do you encourage us, saying that we're songwriters and all, to write any other song than Hare Kṛṣṇa?

Śrīla Prabhupāda: Chanting the Hare Kṛṣṇa mantra is the recommended process for cleaning our hearts. So actually one who chants Hare Kṛṣṇa regularly doesn't have to do anything else. He is already in the correct position. He doesn't have to read any books.

Yoko Ono: Yes, I agree. So why do you say that it's all right to write songs, speak, and all that? It's a waste of time, isn't it?

Śrīla Prabhupāda: No, it's not a waste of time. For instance, Śrī Caitanya Mahāprabhu would spend most of His time simply chanting. He was a *sannyāsī,* a member of the renounced spiritual order of life. So, He was criticized by great *sannyāsīs,* who said, "You have become a *sannyāsī,* and yet You do not read the *Vedānta-sūtra*. You are simply chanting and dancing." In this way, they criticized His constant chanting of Hare Kṛṣṇa. But when Caitanya Mahāprabhu met such stalwart scholars, He did not remain silent. He established the chanting of Hare Kṛṣṇa by sound arguments based on the Vedic scriptures.

Chanting for Liberation

Chanting Hare Kṛṣṇa is sufficient for liberation; there is no doubt about it. But if someone wants to understand the Hare Kṛṣṇa mantra through philosophy, through study, through *Vedānta,* then we do not lack information. We have many books. But it is not that the Hare Kṛṣṇa mantra is somehow insufficient and therefore we are recommending books. The Hare Kṛṣṇa mantra is sufficient. But when Caitanya Mahāprabhu was chanting, He sometimes had to meet opposing scholars, such as Prakāśānanda Sarasvatī and Sārvabhauma Bhaṭṭācārya. And then He was ready to argue with them on the basis of *Vedānta*. So, we should not be dumb. If someone comes to argue with *Vedānta* philosophy, then we must be prepared. When we are preaching, many different types of people will come with questions. We should be able to answer them. Otherwise, the Hare Kṛṣṇa mantra is sufficient. It does not require any education, any reading, or anything else. Simply by chanting Hare Kṛṣṇa, you get the highest perfection. That's a fact.

CHAPTER THREE

Śrīla Prabhupāda Brings the Hare Kṛṣṇa Mantra to the West

When His Divine Grace A. C. Bhaktivedanta Swami Prabhupāda first arrived in America in the midst of the cultural turmoil of the sixties, he quickly captured the hearts and minds of the New York hippies and the San Francisco flower children with the chanting of the Hare Kṛṣṇa mantra.

In 1969 he journeyed to London, and by 1971, Hare Kṛṣṇa had been recorded on hit records by former Beatles John Lennon and George Harrison. By then the mantra had been heard by hundreds of millions of people, and the International Society for Krishna Consciousness, formed in New York in 1966, had spread to six continents. How could an elderly Indian swami in a foreign land, with no money, no support, no friends, and no followers, achieve such phenomenal success? The story that follows includes eyewitness accounts and excerpts from

Śrīla Prabhupāda-līlāmṛta, the authorized biography of this extraordinary saint, written by one of his intimate disciples, Satsvarūpa Dāsa Goswami.

The arduous sea voyage from Calcutta to Boston was finally over. The lone passenger aboard the cargo ship *Jaladuta*, a sixty-nine-year-old Indian holy man, had been given free passage by the owner of the Scindia Steamship Company. His Divine Grace A. C. Bhaktivedanta Swami Prabhupāda arrived at Commonwealth Pier on September 17, 1965.

For thousands of years *kṛṣṇa-bhakti*, love of Kṛṣṇa, had been known only in India, but now, on the order of his spiritual master, Śrīla Prabhupāda had come to awaken the natural, dormant Kṛṣṇa consciousness of the American people.

On his arrival day onboard the *Jaladuta*, he wrote in his diary the following words:

> Absorbed in material life, they [Americans] think themselves very happy and satisfied, and therefore they have no taste for the transcendental message of Vāsudeva [Kṛṣṇa].... But I know that Your causeless mercy can make everything possible, because You are the most expert mystic ... How will I make them understand this message of Kṛṣṇa consciousness? ... O Lord, I am simply praying for Your mercy so that I will be able to convince them about Your message.... I am seeking Your benediction ... I have no devotion, nor do I have any knowledge, but I have strong faith in the holy name of Kṛṣṇa.

In 1922, Śrīla Prabhupāda's spiritual master, His Divine Grace Bhaktisiddhānta Sarasvatī Ṭhākura, had requested him to spread the teachings of Lord Kṛṣṇa, including the Hare Kṛṣṇa mantra, to the West, and now, after a lifetime in preparation, Śrīla Prabhupāda was ready to begin.

After landing in America with the Indian rupee equivalent of eight dollars, he spent his first seven months in the United States with a family in Butler, Pennsylvania, with an Indian yoga teacher in Manhattan, and later, with the help of friends, in a bare rented office in the same part of the city.

By the summer of 1966, he had found a larger location more suited to propagating the Hare Kṛṣṇa *mahā-mantra* and the ancient science of Kṛṣṇa consciousness. That summer Prabhupāda had met a young man named Harvey Cohen, who offered him an old artist-in-residence loft in lower Manhattan's Bowery.

Here, a small group of young Bohemian types would join Śrīla Prabhupāda every Monday, Wednesday, and Friday evening for chanting Hare Kṛṣṇa and classes on the *Bhagavad-gītā*. Although not yet incorporated or known by its present name, the International Society for Krishna Consciousness had been born.

Few of Śrīla Prabhupāda's guests, whose interests included music, drugs, macrobiotics, pacifism, and spiritual meditation, knew very much about what they were chanting or exactly why they were chanting it. They just enjoyed it and liked being in the presence of the man they affectionately called "Swamiji." These musicians, artists, poets, and intellectuals, most of whom had chosen to live outside of mainstream society, felt that by chanting Hare Kṛṣṇa they were taking part in something mystical and unique.

Śrīla Prabhupāda led the solo chanting: Hare Kṛṣṇa, Hare Kṛṣṇa, Kṛṣṇa Kṛṣṇa, Hare Hare/ Hare Rāma, Hare Rāma, Rāma Rāma, Hare Hare. The melody was always the same – a simple four-note phrase, the first four notes of the major scale. Prabhupāda led the *kīrtana* with small three-inch-diameter hand cymbals he had brought with him from India. He would ring them in a one-two-*three,* one-two-*three* fashion. Some of his followers clapped along with him, and some joined in with small finger cymbals of their own. Others sat in yoga postures, hands outstretched, chanting and meditating on this novel transcendental vibration. Guests would sometimes bring other instruments, including guitars, tambouras, flutes, tambourines, and a wide variety of drums.

After a few months some of Śrīla Prabhupāda's followers secured for him a better place to live and spread the chanting of the holy name. The new Second Avenue location on the hippie-filled Lower East Side included an apartment for Śrīla Prabhupāda one floor up and a ground-floor storefront, which he would use as a temple. Within a few weeks, the small sixty-by-twenty-five-foot storefront was packed with young people three nights a week. Gradually the storefront took on the appearance of a temple as visitors began to bring tapestries and paintings for the walls, carpets for the floors, and amplification equipment for Śrīla Prabhupāda's lectures and *kīrtanas*.

Prabhupāda's *kīrtanas* were lively and captivating, with numerous guests spontaneously rising to their feet, clapping and dancing. Śrīla Prabhupāda, always conducting the *kīrtana* (group chanting) in call-and-response fashion and playing a small African bongolike drum, would accelerate the chant faster and faster, until after about half an hour it would reach a climax and suddenly end. Chanting along with Śrīla Prabhupāda in this small room on Second Avenue, guests found themselves transported into another dimension, a spiritual dimension, in which the anxieties and pressures of everyday life in New York City simply did not exist. Many soon caught on that chanting Hare Kṛṣṇa was an intense and effective form of meditation, a direct means of communion with something greater than themselves, no matter what their conception of the Absolute.

Śrīla Prabhupāda initiated his first disciples in September of '66, at which time about a dozen students vowed to chant a minimum of sixteen rounds a day on their beads. This meant reciting the sixteen-word mantra 1,728 times a day, a meditation that would take them between one and a half to two hours to complete.

Prabhupāda's flock soon began to print and distribute invitations and leaflets such as this one:

Practice the transcendental sound vibration,
Hare Krishna, Hare Krishna, Krishna Krishna, Hare Hare
Hare Rāma, Hare Rāma, Rāma Rāma, Hare Hare.
This chanting will cleanse the dust from the
mirror of the mind.

Another invited America's youth to

STAY HIGH FOREVER!
No More Coming Down

Practice Krishna Consciousness
Expand your consciousness by practicing the

* TRANSCENDENTAL SOUND VIBRATION *

HARE KRISHNA, HARE KRISHNA
KRISHNA KRISHNA, HARE HARE
HARE RAMA, HARE RAMA
RAMA RAMA, HARE HARE

In the mornings Śrīla Prabhupāda would lead the devotees in one round of *japa* (chanting on beads). After chanting with Prabhupāda, the devotees would chant their remaining sixteen rounds on their own.

The celebrated American poet Allen Ginsberg, accompanying the *kīrtana* on his harmonium, had by now become a regular at the evening chanting sessions at the temple and in nearby Tompkins Square Park. In a 1980 interview published in Śrīla Prabhupāda's biography, he recalled his experiences.

Allen: *I liked immediately the idea that Swami Bhaktivedanta had chosen the Lower East Side of New York for his practice.... I was astounded that he'd come with the chanting, because it seemed like a reinforcement from India. I had been running around singing Hare Kṛṣṇa but had never understood exactly why or what it meant.... I thought it was great now that he was here to expound on the Hare Kṛṣṇa mantra – that would sort of justify my singing. I knew what I was doing but I didn't have any theological background to satisfy further inquiry, and here was someone who did. So I thought that was absolutely great.... If anyone wanted to know the technical intricacies and the ultimate history, I could send them to him.... he had a personal, selfless sweetness like total devotion. And that was what always conquered me ... a kind of personal charm, coming from dedication ... I always liked to be with him.*

The chanting of Hare Kṛṣṇa seemed to spread in an almost magical way, and as time went on, the number of people attracted to it increased exponentially. Even in this unlikely New York setting, the mantra seemed to have a life of its own. Whether it was the melody, the beat, the sound of the words, the look of the devotees, or Prabhupāda's humility or serenity, nearly everyone who then came in touch with the chanting of Hare Kṛṣṇa responded favorably.

In December 1966, Śrīla Prabhupāda would explain on his first record album, the LP that introduced two of the Beatles, John Lennon and George Harrison, to Hare Kṛṣṇa, that "the chanting Hare Kṛṣṇa, Hare Kṛṣṇa, Kṛṣṇa Kṛṣṇa, Hare Hare/ Hare Rāma, Hare Rāma, Rāma Rāma, Hare Hare is not a material sound vibration, but comes directly from the spiritual world."

Prabhupāda's Tompkins Square Park *kīrtanas* were spiritual happenings that are now legendary. Hundreds of people from all walks of life took part; some as observers and some as eager participants, chanting, clapping their hands, dancing, and playing musical instruments. Irving

Halpern, one of many local musicians who regularly participated, remembers the scene.

Irving: *The park resounded. The musicians were very careful in listening to the mantras. . . . I have talked to a couple of musicians about it, and we agreed that in his head this Swami must have had hundreds and hundreds of melodies that had been brought back from the real learning from the other side of the world. So many people came there just to tune in to the musical gift, the transmission of the dharma. "Hey," they would say, "listen to this holy monk."*

People were really sure there were going to be unusual feats, grandstanding, flashy levitations, or whatever people expected was going to happen. But when the simplicity of what the Swami was really saying, when you began to sense it – whether you were motivated to actually make a lifetime commitment and go this way of life, or whether you merely wanted to place it in a place and give certain due respect to it – it turned you around.

And that was interesting, too, the different ways in which people regarded the kīrtana. *Some people thought it was a prelude. Some people thought it was a main event. Some people liked the music. Some people liked the poetic sound of it.*

After the *kīrtanas* Śrīla Prabhupāda usually spoke for a few minutes about Kṛṣṇa consciousness, inviting everyone back to the temple for a Sunday afternoon "love festival" of chanting and feasting, a weekly event that soon became a tradition that continues today. The October 10 edition of the *New York Times* described the Tompkins Square Park *kīrtana* with the following headline: "Swami's Flock Chants In Park To Find Ecstasy."

> Sitting under a tree in a Lower East Side park and occasionally dancing, fifty followers of a Hindu swami repeated a sixteen-word chant for two hours yesterday afternoon to the accompaniment of cymbals, tambourines, sticks, drums, bells, and a small

> reed organ.... Repetition of the chant, Swami A.C. Bhaktivedanta says, is the best way to achieve self-realization in this age of destruction.
>
> [M]any in the crowd of about a hundred persons standing around the chanters found themselves swaying to or clapping hands in time to the hypnotic rhythmic music. "It brings a state of ecstasy," said Allen Ginsberg the poet. "The ecstasy of the chant or mantra Hare Krishna, Hare Krishna, Krishna Krishna, Hare Hare/ Hare Rama, Hare Rama, Rama Rama, Hare Hare has replaced LSD and other drugs for many of the Swami's followers."

At the same time, New York's avant-garde newspaper *The East Village Other* ran a front-page story with a full-page photograph of Śrīla Prabhupāda standing and speaking to a large group of people in the park. The banner headline read "SAVE EARTH NOW!!" and in large type just below the picture, the *mahā-mantra* was printed: "HARE KRISHNA HARE KRISHNA KRISHNA KRISHNA HARE HARE HARE RAMA HARE RAMA RAMA RAMA HARE HARE." The article admired the chanting and described how Śrīla Prabhupāda "had succeeded in convincing the world's toughest audience – Bohemians, acidheads, potheads, and hippies – that he knew the way to God."

> Turn Off, Sing Out, and Fall In. This new brand of holy man, with all due deference to Dr. Leary, has come forth with a brand of "Consciousness Expansion" that's sweeter than acid, cheaper than pot, and non-bustible by fuzz.

The newspaper story described how a visit to the temple at 26 Second Avenue would bring "living, visible, tangible proof" that God is alive and well. The story quoted one of Śrīla Prabhupāda's new disciples:

> I started chanting to myself, like the Swami said, when I was walking down the street – Hare Krishna, Hare Krishna, Krishna Krishna, Hare Hare/ Hare Rama, Hare Rama, Rama Rama, Hare Hare – over and over, and suddenly everything started looking so beautiful, the kids, the old men and women ... even the creeps looked beautiful ... to say nothing of the trees and flowers.

Finding it superior to the euphoria from any kind of drug, he said,

> There's no coming down from this. I can always do this any time, anywhere. It is always with you.

To San Francisco and Beyond

Early in 1967, several of Śrīla Prabhupāda's disciples left New York and opened a temple in the heart of San Francisco's Haight-Ashbury district, home for thousands of hippies and "flower children" from all over the country. Within a short time, Śrīla Prabhupāda's temple there had become a spiritual haven for troubled, searching, and sometimes desperate young people. Drug overdoses were common, and hundreds of confused, dazed, and disenchanted young Americans roamed the streets.

Haridāsa, the first president of the San Francisco temple, remembers what it was like.

Haridāsa: *The hippies needed all the help they could get, and they knew it. And the Rādhā-Kṛṣṇa temple was certainly a kind of spiritual haven. Kids sensed it. They were running, living on the streets, no place where they could go, where they could rest, where people weren't going to hurt them.*

I think it saved a lot of lives; there might have been a lot more casualties if it hadn't been for Hare Kṛṣṇa. It was like opening a temple in a battlefield. It was the hardest place to do it, but it was the place where it was most needed. Although the Swami had no precedents for dealing with any of this, he applied the chanting with miraculous results. The chanting was wonderful. It worked.

Michael Bowen, an artist and one of the leading figures of the Haight-Ashbury scene, recalled that Śrīla Prabhupāda had "an amazing ability to get people off drugs, especially speed, heroin, burnt-out LSD cases – all of that."

Every day at the temple devotees cooked and served to over two hundred young people a free, sumptuous multi-course lunch of vegetarian food offered to Kṛṣṇa. Many local merchants helped to make this possible by donating to the cause. An early San Francisco devotee recalls those days.

Harṣarāṇī: *People who were plain lost or needed comforting ... sort of wandered or staggered into the temple. Some of them stayed and became devotees, and some just took* prasāda *[spiritual food] and left. Just from a medical standpoint, doctors didn't know what to do with people on LSD. The police and the free clinics in the area couldn't handle the overload of people taking LSD. The police saw Swamiji [Śrīla Prabhupāda] as a certain refuge.*

Throughout lunch, devotees played the New York recording of Śrīla Prabhupāda chanting the Hare Kṛṣṇa mantra. The sacred sound reinforced the spiritual mood of the temple and helped to ease the tensions and frustrations of its young guests.

Sunday, January 29, 1967 marked the major spiritual event of the San Francisco hippie era, and Śrīla Prabhupāda, who was ready to go anywhere to spread Kṛṣṇa consciousness, was there. The Grateful Dead, Moby Grape, Janis Joplin and Big Brother and the Holding Company, Jefferson Airplane, Quicksilver Messenger Service – all the new-wave San Francisco bands – had agreed to appear with Śrīla Prabhupāda at the Avalon Ballroom's Mantra-Rock Dance, proceeds from which would go to the local Hare Kṛṣṇa temple.

Thousands of hippies, anticipating an exciting evening, packed the hall. LSD pioneer Timothy Leary dutifully paid the standard $2.50 admission fee and entered the ballroom, followed by Augustus Owsley Stanley II, known for his own brand of LSD.

At about 10:00 PM, Śrīla Prabhupāda and a small entourage of devotees arrived amid uproarious applause and cheering by a crowd that had waited weeks in great anticipation for this moment. Śrīla Prabhupāda was given a seat of honor onstage and was introduced by Allen Ginsberg, who explained his own realizations about the Hare Kṛṣṇa *mahā-mantra* and how it had spread from the small storefront in New York to San Francisco. The well-known poet told the crowd that the chanting of the Hare Kṛṣṇa mantra in the early morning at the Rādhā-Kṛṣṇa temple was an important community service to those who were "coming down from LSD," because the chanting would "stabilize their consciousness on reentry."

The chanting started slowly but rhythmically, and little by little it spread throughout the ballroom, enveloping everyone. Hippies got to their feet, held hands, and began to dance as enormous, pulsing pictures of Kṛṣṇa were projected around the walls of the ballroom in perfect sync with the beat of the mantra. By the time Śrīla Prabhupāda stood and began to dance with his arms raised, the crowd was completely absorbed in chanting, dancing, and playing small musical instruments they had brought for the occasion.

Ginsberg later recalled, "We sang Hare Kṛṣṇa all evening. It was absolutely great – an open thing. It was the height of the Haight-Ashbury spiritual enthusiasm."

As the tempo speeded up, the chanting and dancing became more and more intense, spurred on by a stageful of top rock musicians, who were as charmed by the magic of the *mahā-mantra* as the amateur musicians had been at the Tompkins Square *kīrtanas* only a few weeks before.

The chant rose; it seemed to surge and swell without limit. When it seemed it could go no further, the chanting stopped. Śrīla Prabhupāda offered prayers to his spiritual master into the microphone and ended by saying three times, "All glories to the assembled devotees!" The Haight-Ashbury neighborhood buzzed with talk of the Mantra-Rock Dance for weeks afterward.

Within a few months of the Mantra-Rock event, devotees in San Francisco, New York, and Montreal began to take to the streets with their *mṛdaṅgas* (clay drums) and *karatālas* (hand cymbals) to chant the *mahā-mantra* on a daily basis. In just a few years, temples were opening all over North America and Europe, and people everywhere were hearing the chanting of Hare Kṛṣṇa.

On May 31, 1969, when the Vietnam War protest movement was reaching its climax, six devotees joined John Lennon and Yoko Ono in their Montreal hotel room to play instruments and sing on John and Yoko's famous recording "Give Peace a Chance." This song, which included the mantra, and a hit single, "The Hare Krishna Mantra," produced in September of the same year by Beatle George Harrison and featuring the devotees, introduced millions to the chanting. Even Broadway's long-running musical hit *Hair* included exuberant choruses of the Hare Kṛṣṇa mantra.

At the now historic mass antiwar demonstration in Washington, DC, on November 15, 1969, devotees from all over the United States and Canada chanted the Hare Kṛṣṇa mantra throughout the day and distributed "The Peace Formula," a small leaflet based on Śrīla Prabhupāda's teachings from the Vedic scriptures. "The Peace Formula," which proposed a spiritual solution to the problem of war, was distributed en masse for many months and influenced thousands of lives.

By 1970, when George Harrison's "My Sweet Lord" – with its beautiful recurring lyrics of Hare Kṛṣṇa and Hare Rāma – was the international number-one hit song of the day, devotees in *dhotīs* and saris, chanting the *mahā-mantra* with musical instruments, were now a familiar sight in almost every major city throughout the world. Because of Śrīla Prabhupāda's deep love for Lord Kṛṣṇa and his own spiritual master, his amazing determination, and his sincere compassion, "Hare Kṛṣṇa" had become a household word.

CHAPTER FOUR

Chanting for Higher Consciousness: A Cultural History

It's a scene that has been repeated countless times on the thoroughfares of cities throughout the Western world – from Hollywood Boulevard in L.A. to Fifth Avenue in New York, from Oxford Street in London to the Champs Élysées in Paris. There, in the midst of traffic, shops, restaurants, and movie theaters, people suddenly find themselves confronted by a group of young persons singing and dancing to the beat of cylindrical drums and the brassy cadence of hand cymbals. The men are dressed in flowing robes and have shaven heads; the women wear colorful Indian saris. Of course, it's the Hare Kṛṣṇa people, chanting their now familiar mantra, Hare Kṛṣṇa, Hare Kṛṣṇa ... But what's actually going on? Is it some form of protest, avant-garde street theater, a religious demonstration, or what?

If you were to ask them, you'd learn that these people are performing a type of meditation long encouraged and practiced in the West – the chanting of the holy names of God. (Kṛṣṇa is the Sanskrit name for the Supreme Lord.) Of course, meditation is a word that's thrown around quite loosely these days. It's come to mean practically any technique employed to silence and calm the harried modern mind. But the ancient and authorized form of meditation practiced by Hare Kṛṣṇa people has a much deeper and more sublime purpose. Although it easily soothes the turbulent mind, it also awakens those who chant it to their original, joyful spiritual nature and consciousness, imparting a genuine sense of pleasure unavailable by any other means.

The *Vedas,* scriptures containing the timeless spiritual knowledge of ancient India, state that such an awakening process is desperately needed because everyone in this material world is in a sleeping, dreamlike condition. We have forgotten our original, spiritual identity, accepting instead a temporary material body composed of physical elements as our real self.

The *Vedas* compare the material body to the subtle forms we experience in dreams. While sleeping, we forget our normal waking identity and may find ourselves enjoying or suffering in different types of bodies. But when we hear the ringing of the alarm clock, we awaken and return to normal consciousness. We remember who we are and what we should be doing. Similarly, by hearing the powerful transcendental sound vibrations of the Hare Kṛṣṇa mantra, we can gradually wake up to our original self, the soul, which is characterized by eternality and is full of knowledge and ever-increasing pleasure.

The sages of ancient India therefore tell us that the goal of human life should not be to try to enjoy our temporary dreamlike situation in the material world. Rather, we are advised to awaken to our original, spiritual nature and ultimately return to our true home in the spiritual world, where we may enjoy an eternal relationship with the Supreme Personality of Godhead, Lord Kṛṣṇa.

This search for the true self through the meditative process is not something recently discovered, nor is it in any way alien to the basically rationalistic philosophical and spiritual traditions of the West. Although Western civilization has for the most part directed its energies outward in various efforts to control and exploit the resources of nature, there have always been inward-directed philosophers, saints, and mystics who have dedicated themselves to a higher purpose than material well-being, which is in all cases temporary.

The Search for the Self

The Greek philosophers Socrates and Plato held a view of man's original nature quite similar to that of the Vedic sages. This temporary world, they taught, is not our real home; we once existed in a spiritual world. In Plato's famous dialogues, Socrates says that in our original condition "We were pure ourselves and not yet enshrined in that living tomb which we carry about, now that we are imprisoned in the body like an oyster in his shell.[1] The purpose of philosophy, for these early Athenian thinkers, was to awaken a person to his original, spiritual identity, now hidden within the covering of the physical body.

The very same thing was taught in Galilee four hundred years later by Jesus Christ. In the Gospel of St. John, Christ says, "It is the spirit that quickeneth, the flesh profiteth nothing."[2] In other words, the body is simply an external covering for the soul, which is the real life-giving force. Therefore, Jesus warned, "What profiteth a man if he gain the whole world but lose his immortal soul?"[3] The highest goal of life, Christ taught, is to understand and experience our inner, spiritual nature. In the Gospel of St. Luke, Jesus instructs humankind to look within for true spiritual life:

"Neither shall they say, Lo here! or lo there! for behold, the kingdom of God is within you."[4]

Describing his inner search for God through meditation, St. Augustine, great saint and eminent philosopher of the Roman Catholic Church, tells us in *Confessions* how his mind "withdrew its thoughts from experience, abstracting itself from the contradictory throng of sensuous images."[5]

During the Middle Ages in Europe, there was widespread interest in meditation, with many saints and philosophers writing of their thoughts about the inner quest for divine reality. Thomas à Kempis, in his classic *Imitation of Christ*, cautions us about material life and summarizes the purpose and goal of meditation: "What do you seek here, since this world is not your resting place" Your true home is in Heaven; therefore remember that all things of this world are transitory. All things are passing and yourself with them. See that you do not cling to them, lest you become entangled and perish with them. Let all your thoughts be with the Most High."[6]

When one achieves this deep spiritual vision, his entire worldview is completely transformed, as in the case of St. Francis of Assisi, who devoted his life to prayer and meditation. In his *Life of St. Francis* St. Bonaventure writes, "In all fair things, he beheld Him who is most fair, and, through the traces of Him which He has implanted in all His creatures, he was led on to reach the All-loved, constructing of these things a ladder whereby he might ascend to Him who is Loveliness itself."[7] In other words, when one's original, spiritual consciousness is revived, one sees God everywhere and in everything. One enters a unique world of spiritual knowledge and pleasure, far superior to what most of us perceive as reality – a spiritual reality that lies just beyond our ordinary abilities of perception. William James, the American philosopher who specialized in the psychology of religion, writing on this point, said, "Our normal waking consciousness, rational consciousness as we call it, is but one special type of consciousness, whilst all about it, parted from it by the filmiest of screens, there lie potential forms of consciousness entirely different. We may go throughout life without suspecting their existence, but apply the requisite stimulus, and at a touch they are there in all their completeness."[8]

But what is the "requisite stimulus" for awakening the dormant consciousness of the self and God that lies within everyone's heart? All genuine spiritual authorities agree that such transcendental experiences cannot be awakened by any material stimulus or experience, including the ingestion of "mind-expanding" or "mind-altering" drugs.

When Śrīla Prabhupāda was asked by a follower of Timothy Leary about LSD's place in a person's spiritual life, Śrīla Prabhupāda said that drugs were not necessary for spiritual life, that they could not produce spiritual consciousness, and that all drug-induced "religious visions" were simply hallucinations. To realize God was not so easy or cheap that one could do it just by taking a pill or smoking.[9]

Sound and Self-Realization

The Vedic scriptures advise that the proper technique for awakening spiritual consciousness is the hearing and chanting of transcendental sounds or mantras, like the Hare Kṛṣṇa mantra. The power of sound to effect changes in consciousness has long been recognized. The English philosopher and statesman Sir Francis Bacon noted that "the sense of hearing striketh the spirit more immediately than any other senses."[10]

Ordinary *material* sounds, however, will not awaken spiritual consciousness. For this one must hear *spiritual* sound vibrations. Therefore, almost every religion in the world recommends that we meditate on the word of God. St. John wrote in his Gospel, "In the beginning was the Word, and the Word was with God, and the Word was God."[11] Divine sound is thus of a vastly different quality than worldly or material sound. This fact was clearly explained by St. Augustine in his *Confessions*. Once, as he emerged from a mystic trance, he said he "heard again the babble of our own tongues, wherein each word has a beginning and an ending. Far unlike Thy Word, our Lord, who abideth in Himself, never growing old and making all things new."[12] And in the Gospel of St. John Christ says, "The words that I speak unto you, they are spirit."[13]

While the word or teachings of God have enormous power to transform and uplift our lives, the actual names of God are just as important when they are praised aloud in song or quietly meditated on. Since God is fully spiritual and absolute, the Vedic scriptures inform us that His holy names are invested with the Lord's full spiritual potencies. God and His name are the same. India's *Padma Purāṇa* states, "There is no difference between the holy name of the Lord and the Lord Himself. As such, the holy name is as perfect as the Lord Himself." The Stoic philosopher Maximus noted, "There is one supreme God who is, as it were, the God and mighty father of all." "It is Him," he said, "whom we worship under many names."[14] Modern Jewish theologian Martin Buber also agreed: "All God's names are hallowed."[15]

And the Bible is replete with similar statements. In the Old Testament it is said, "The name of the Lord is a strong tower: the righteous runneth into it and is safe."[16] In Psalms, King David proclaims, "I will praise the name of God with a song."[17] Indeed, the Psalms contain many references to the name of God: "All nations whom Thou hast made shall come and worship before Thee, O Lord: and shall glorify Thy name.[18] ... O give thanks unto the Lord: call upon His name: make known His deeds among the people. Sing unto Him, sing psalms unto Him: talk ye of all His wondrous works. Glory ye in His holy name.[19] ... Praise Him with the timbrel and dance: praise Him with stringed instruments and organs. Praise Him upon the loud cymbals."[20] The prophet Isaiah described God as "One that inhabiteth eternity, and whose name is Holy."[21] Centuries later, Israel Baal Shem Tov (1699–1761), the great Jewish mystic, founded Hasidism, a popular pietistic movement within Judaism, in which members dance and chant in glorification of the Supreme Lord.

Christ, when teaching his disciples how to pray, glorified the Lord's holy name: "Our Father, who art in Heaven, hallowed be Thy name." And in his Epistle to the Romans St. Paul wrote, "For whosoever shall call upon the name of the Lord shall be saved."[22]

In the early Christian churches, there was, according to the historian Eusebius, "one common consent in chanting forth the praises of God."[23] The Gregorian chants, popularized in the sixth century by Pope Gregory the Great and later by works like Handel's masterpiece *Messiah,* with its resounding choruses of *hallelujah* ("praised be the Lord"), are still performed and appreciated all over the world.

In addition to praising the Lord's name and glories in song, there also developed in the Christian churches the practice of meditating on God by chanting prayers on rosary beads, a tradition continued today by millions of Catholics worldwide. John Chrysostom, a saint of the Greek Orthodox Church, especially recommended the "prayerful invocation of the name of God," which he said should be practiced "uninterrupted."[24]

The repetition of the Jesus prayer ("Lord Jesus, Son of God, have mercy on me") became a regular practice among members of the Eastern Church. In *The Way of a Pilgrim,* a Russian monk describes this form of meditation: "The continuous interior prayer of Jesus is a constant uninterrupted calling upon the divine name of Jesus with the lips, in the spirit, in the heart.... One who accustoms himself to this appeal experiences as a result so deep a consolation and so great a need to offer the prayer always, that he can no longer live without it."[25]

Among the followers of Islam, the names of God (Allah) are held sacred and meditated on. According to tradition, there are ninety-nine names of Allah, called "the Beautiful Names." They are found inscribed on monuments such as the Taj Mahal and on the walls of mosques. These names are chanted on an Islamic rosary, which consists of three sets of thirty-three beads. Worshipers repeat the names to help them concentrate their minds on Allah. The words Bismillah al-Rahman al-Rahim, meaning "God the most gracious, God the most the compassionate," are invoked at the beginning of each chapter of the Koran. Other Arabic names of God glorify Him as the creator, provider, and king.

In India the Sikhs place special emphasis on the name of God. Indeed, the Sikhs call God Nāma – "the name." Guru Nanak, founder of the Sikh religion, prayed, "In the ambrosial hours of the morn I meditate on the grace of the true name," and said that he was instructed by the Lord in a vision to "Go and repeat My name, and cause others to do likewise."[26]

"Rosaries are widely used in Buddhism; large ones by monks, smaller ones by the laity," says Geoffrey Parrinder, a professor of comparative religion at the University of London, in his book *Worship in the World's Religions*. "The large ones have 108 beads, the two halves representing the fifty-four stages of becoming a Boddhisattva (enlightened one). The large bead in the middle stands for Buddha."

Members of Japan's largest Buddhist order, the Pure Land sect, practice repetition of the name of Buddha (*namu amida butsu*). The founder, Shinran Shonin, says, "The virtue of the holy name, the gift of him that is enlightened, is spread throughout the world."[27] The Buddhist teachings reveal that by chanting the name of Buddha the worshiper

His Divine Grace A. C. Bhaktivedanta Swami Prabhupāda, Founder-*Ācārya* (spiritual master) of the International Society for Krishna Consciousness, leads meditative singing of the Hare Kṛṣṇa *mahā-mantra*.

Lord Kṛṣṇa, the Supreme Personality of Godhead. In the *Bhagavad-gītā*, Lord Kṛṣṇa explains to his friend Arjuna, "If one offers me with love and devotion a leaf, a flower, fruit, or water, I will accept it."

George Harrison and the members of the Radha Krishna Temple group listening to the playback of their soon-to-be hit, "Hare Krishna Mantra," at Apple's Abbey Road Studios on July 7, 1969.

George Harrison chants Hare Kṛṣṇa with the London devotees. You can just see Mukunda on the left.

George Harrison, John Lennon, and Yoko Ono waiting in their garden at Tittenhurst Park to meet Śrīla Prabhupāda.

The poster that advertised San Francisco's major spiritual happening of the 1960s: The Mantra-Rock Dance at the Avalon Ballroom, featuring Śrīla Prabhupāda, Allen Ginsberg, and the most popular new rock bands of the day.

George Harrison and Pattie Boyd with Śrīla Prabhupāda and a disciple at George's home in England, 1969.

Śrīla Prabhupāda talks with disciples on the lawn of Bhaktivedanta Manor, the Tudor mansion in Hertfordshire donated to the Hare Kṛṣṇa movement by George Harrison. Over the years it has developed into a thriving spiritual center.

George Harrison and Mukunda (with record cover) at the Sydenham Hill press launch of the "Hare Krishna Mantra" 45-rpm single.

Ratha-yātrā is the Hare Kṛṣṇa movement's biggest street festival. Celebrated yearly in cities around the UK, crowds pull the three huge wooden chariots by hand.

Throughout the festival participants joyfully sing the Hare Kṛṣṇa mantra and dance to the beating of drums and chiming of hand cymbals. The procession ends with a stage show, festival, and delicious vegetarian *prasāda* feast.

becomes liberated from the cycle of reincarnation and joins the Buddha in the Pure Land, or spiritual world.

Kṛṣṇa: The All-Encompassing Name of God

Although God is known throughout the world by many different names, each of which describes some particular aspect of His glories and attractive features, there is one name that expresses the sum total of God's infinite qualities and characteristics. This supreme, all-encompassing, and most powerful name of God is found in the oldest religious scriptures in the world, the Sanskrit *Vedas* of India, which state that the principal name of God is Kṛṣṇa.

Śrīla Prabhupāda explains: "When we speak of Kṛṣṇa, we refer to God. There are many names for God throughout the world and throughout the universe, but Kṛṣṇa is the supreme name according to Vedic knowledge."[28] He further states, "God has many names according to His activities, but because He possesses so many opulences, and because with these opulences He attracts everyone, He is called Kṛṣṇa ['all-attractive']."[29]

The spiritual qualities of Kṛṣṇa's holy name are described throughout the Vedic literatures. The *Padma Purāṇa* states, "The holy name of Kṛṣṇa is transcendentally blissful. It bestows all spiritual benedictions, for it is Kṛṣṇa Himself, the reservoir of all pleasure.... It is not a material name under any condition, and it is no less powerful than Kṛṣṇa Himself. Since Kṛṣṇa's name is not contaminated by the material qualities, there is no question of its being involved with illusion. Kṛṣṇa's name is always liberated and spiritual; it is never conditioned by the laws of material nature. This is because the name of Kṛṣṇa and Kṛṣṇa Himself are identical."

Since time immemorial, millions of devotees and saintly persons have chanted the name of Kṛṣṇa to achieve spiritual perfection. But history records that it was widely popularized by Lord Caitanya, an incarnation of Lord Kṛṣṇa who appeared in Bengal some five centuries ago and established the chanting of the Hare Kṛṣṇa mantra as the universal spiritual practice for the present age.

According to Vedic cosmology, the material creation eternally passes through cycles of four ages. Each begins with a golden age (Satya-yuga), then conditions progressively deteriorate, ending in Kali-yuga, an age characterized by quarrel and hypocrisy. For each of the four ages the *Vedas* prescribe a universal method of self-realization just suited for that particular age.

For instance, in Satya-yuga the recommended path is mystic yoga, which involves a lifetime of unbroken yoga practice accompanied by strict vows of penance and austerity. We are presently near the beginning of the last age, Kali-yuga. In this age people no longer have the endurance, willpower, or life span necessary to successfully practice the original yoga system described in the *Vedas*. The Vedic scriptures therefore advise: "For spiritual progress in this Age of Kali, there is no alternative, no alternative, no alternative to chanting the holy name, the holy name, the holy name of the Lord."[30]

The *Kali-santaraṇa Upaniṣad* specifically recommends the chanting of the Hare Kṛṣṇa mantra: "Hare Kṛṣṇa, Hare Kṛṣṇa, Kṛṣṇa Kṛṣṇa, Hare Hare/ Hare Rāma, Hare Rāma, Rāma Rāma, Hare Hare – these sixteen names composed of thirty-two syllables are the only means to counteract the evil effects of Kali-yuga. In all the *Vedas* it is seen that to cross the ocean of nescience there is no alternative to chanting the holy name."

Lord Caitanya's biographers record that He spent many years traveling all over India spreading the chanting of the holy names of Kṛṣṇa. He chanted the Hare Kṛṣṇa mantra congregationally (*kīrtana*) to the accompaniment of musical instruments, including drums and hand cymbals. The

Lord also chanted the mantra quietly a specific number of times daily as a private meditation (*japa*). In the *Śikṣāṣṭaka,* His famous prayers about the holy names of Kṛṣṇa, Lord Caitanya wrote, "Let there be all victory for the chanting of the holy name of Lord Kṛṣṇa, which can cleanse the mirror of the heart and stop the miseries of the blazing fire of material existence. That chanting is the waxing moon that spreads the white lotus of good fortune for all living entities. It is the life and soul of all education. The chanting of the holy name of Kṛṣṇa expands the blissful ocean of transcendental life. It gives a cooling effect to everyone and enables one to taste full nectar at every step."

During His lifetime, Lord Caitanya predicted that the holy names of Kṛṣṇa would spread to every town and village in the world. This prophecy lay unfulfilled for four hundred years, until the time of Bhaktivinoda Ṭhākura, a great spiritual master in direct disciplic succession from Lord Caitanya. In 1885 Bhaktivinoda wrote: "Lord Caitanya did not advent Himself to liberate only a few men in India. Rather, His main objective was to emancipate all living entities of all countries throughout the entire universe and preach the eternal religion.... There is no doubt that this unquestionable order will come to pass.... Very soon the unparalleled path of the congregational chanting of the Lord's holy name will be propagated all over the world.... Oh, for that day when the fortunate English, French, Russian, German, and American people will take up banners, drums, and hand cymbals and raise *kīrtana* through their streets and towns! When will that day come?"[31]

Bhaktivinoda's vision became a reality in less than a century. In 1965, India's greatest spiritual and cultural ambassador, His Divine Grace A. C. Bhaktivedanta Swami Prabhupāda, arrived in New York's East Village, the heart of the countercultural movement of the sixties. Within a year Śrīla Prabhupāda, tenth in the line of spiritual masters from Lord Caitanya, had founded the International

Society for Krishna Consciousness. Very quickly the sound of the chanting of Hare Kṛṣṇa spread, first across America, then on to England and throughout the world.

The Vedic scriptures predict that although the Age of Kali is the most degraded of all, the chanting of the Hare Kṛṣṇa mantra will dramatically alter the present war-torn, hate-filled atmosphere of the world. These most ancient, timeless writings forecast a golden age, beginning with the widespread chanting of Hare Kṛṣṇa, during which the painful disturbances of this age will gradually be mitigated and people everywhere will be economically, politically, socially, culturally, and spiritually happy.

Śrīla Prabhupāda explains, "Kali-yuga continues for 432,000 years, of which only 5,000 years have passed. Thus there is still a balance of 427,000 years to come. Of these 427,000 years, the 10,000 years of the *saṅkīrtana* movement* inaugurated by Śrī Caitanya Mahāprabhu 500 years ago provide the opportunity for the fallen souls of Kali-yuga to take to the Kṛṣṇa consciousness movement, chant the Hare Kṛṣṇa *mahā-mantra,* and thus be delivered from the clutches of material existence and return home, back to Godhead."[32]

* The movement to spread the congregational chanting of God's names.

Notes

1. *Phaedrus,* translated by Benjamin Jowett.
2. John 6:63.
3. Mark 8:36.
4. Luke 17:21.
5. *Confessions,* translated by C. Bigge.
   London: Methuen and Company, Ltd., p. 244.
6. *Imitation of Christ,* translated by Leo Sherley-Price.
   Baltimore: Penguin Classics edition.
7. *The Life of St. Francis.* New York: Everyman's Library, 1912.
8. *The Varieties of Religious Experience,* William James.
   London: Longman, Green, and Co., p. 388.
9. *Śrīla Prabhupāda-līlāmṛta,* Satsvarūpa dāsa Goswami.
   Los Angeles: Bhaktivedanta Book Trust, 1980, p. 201.
10. *Sylva sylvarum,* in *Works,* ed. James Spedding, et. al.
    New York: 1864, IV, p. 231.
11. John 1:1
12. *Confessions,* X, p. 321.
13. John 6:63
14. *Comparative Religion,* Esther Carpenter, 1913, p. 35.
15. *Worship in the World's Religions,* Geoffrey Parrinder.
    London: Faber and Faber, 1961, p. 7.
16. Proverbs 18:10
17. Psalms 69:30
18. Psalms 86:9
19. Psalms 105:1–4
20. Psalms 150:4–5
21. Isaiah 57:15
22. Romans 10:13
23. *Ecclesiastical History.*
24. *The Way of a Pilgrim,* translator R. M. French.
    London: Society for Promoting Christian Knowledge.
25. Ibid.
26. *Japji* (The meditations of Guru Nanak).
27. *Buddhist Psalms,* Yamabe, S., and Beck, L. A. Murray, 1921, p. 86.
28. *Śrī Nāmāmṛta: The Nectar of the Holy Name,*
    Los Angeles: Bhaktivedanta Book Trust, 1982, p. 142.
29. Ibid.
30. *Bṛhan-nāradīya Purāṇa.*
31. *Sajjana-toṣaṇī.*
32. *Śrī Nāmāmṛta,* p. 249.

CHAPTER FIVE

The Life of Śrī Caitanya

In the latter part of the fifteenth century, India's most extraordinary political, cultural, and religious reformer appeared in a small town in West Bengal.

Five hundred years before Gandhi, this remarkable personality inaugurated a massive nonviolent civil disobedience movement. He swept aside the stifling restrictions of the hereditary caste system and made it possible for people from any station in life to achieve the highest platform of spiritual enlightenment. In doing so He broke the stranglehold of a proud intellectual elite on India's religious life. Ignoring all kinds of outmoded rituals and formulas, He introduced a revolutionary spiritual movement that was rapidly accepted all over India – a movement which, because of its universal appeal, has now spread all over the world. The name of this powerful reformer was Śrī Kṛṣṇa Caitanya Mahāprabhu, the founder of the modern-day Hare Kṛṣṇa movement.

The Vedic scriptures of India had long predicted His birth, which occurred in 1486 in Māyāpur, a quarter of the city of Navadvīpa. Great saints and scholars soon detected that He was not an ordinary human being but the Supreme Personality of Godhead Himself, Lord Kṛṣṇa, appearing as a great devotee of the Lord.

Śrī Caitanya had little patience with ritualistic religious functions, and as He grew to young manhood, He began to carry out His divine mission. He wanted all people everywhere to have access to the actual experience of love of God, by which one can feel the highest spiritual ecstasies. This awakening, Śrī Caitanya taught, could be attained by *saṅkīrtana* – the chanting of the holy names of God, the Hare Kṛṣṇa mantra.

Śrī Caitanya rapidly acquired many followers, who immediately took up the chanting, sometimes performing it in their homes and sometimes in the streets of Navadvīpa. Śrī Caitanya Mahāprabhu's *saṅkīrtana* movement immediately threatened the established groups in the social hierarchy – the Muslim rulers of Bengal and the hereditary Hindu priestly class, the caste priests who were attempting to artificially monopolize religious leadership. Members of both groups lodged complaints with the local Muslim ruler, Chand Kazi.

Agreeing that Śrī Caitanya and His followers threatened the established order the Kazi tried to suppress the growing *saṅkīrtana* movement. On his order constables raided the home of one of Śrī Caitanya's followers and smashed the drums used in the chanting. The Kazi ordered that the chanting be immediately stopped, and he threatened that if it began again in Navadvīpa, he would be ruthless with those responsible.

When informed of the raid, Śrī Caitanya immediately organized the largest peaceful civil disobedience movement in Indian history up to that time. On a prearranged evening, Śrī Caitanya and one hundred thousand of His followers suddenly appeared in the streets of Navadvīpa and divided into many well-organized chanting parties. As they danced through the city, the sound of the Hare Kṛṣṇa mantra resounded in a deafening roar. Finally, the chanters converged on the residence of the Kazi, who hid inside.

At Śrī Caitanya's invitation, however, the Kazi appeared, and the two began negotiations. Speaking politely, and with great logic and reason, Śrī Caitanya convinced the Kazi that the complaints against *saṅkīrtana* were groundless. In a dramatic conversion, the Kazi himself became a follower of Śrī Caitanya and actively promoted and protected the *saṅkīrtana* movement. To this very day Hindus visit the tomb of this Muslim magistrate to pay their respects. Since the time of the Kazi, the Muslim inhabitants of Navadvīpa have never interfered with the public chanting of the Hare Kṛṣṇa mantra, even during the time of the Hindu-Muslim riots.

Not long after this important victory in His native town, Śrī Caitanya began to spread His movement all over India. For six years He traveled the length and breadth of the country, chanting the Hare Kṛṣṇa mantra and spreading love of God. At many places, crowds of hundreds of thousands of people would join with Him in massive chanting parties. Nevertheless, He also encountered opponents, the strongest of whom were the Māyāvādīs, an elitist group of philosophers who had spread throughout India, twisting the meaning of the Vedic scriptures in a vain attempt to prove that God has no personality or form. The impersonalists also believed that spiritual enlightenment could be obtained only by a chosen few who knew Sanskrit and arduously studied the *Vedānta-sūtra*.

Throughout His travels, Śrī Caitanya struggled against the Māyāvādīs and succeeded in convincing many of them by the strength of His preaching. One of the greatest philosophers of the Māyāvāda school, Sārvabhauma

Bhaṭṭācārya, tried to prevail over Śrī Caitanya in philosophical discussion but was defeated. Countering the Bhaṭṭācārya's impersonal explanation of God, Śrī Caitanya said, "The living entities are all individual persons, and they are all parts and parcels of the Supreme Whole. If the parts and parcels are individual persons, the source of their emanation must not be impersonal. He is the Supreme Person among all relative persons." Then out of His causeless mercy, Śrī Caitanya performed a wondrous miracle, manifesting before Sārvabhauma Bhaṭṭācārya His beautiful, original, spiritual form as Kṛṣṇa, the Supreme Personality of Godhead. Falling at Lord Caitanya's feet, the former impersonalist philosopher surrendered to Him and soon became a great devotee of the Lord.

But the biggest confrontation with the Māyāvādīs was yet to come, and it occurred in the city that had for centuries been the capital of the Māyāvāda school, Benares. There Lord Caitanya stayed with His friends and devotees and continued His *saṅkīrtana* movement, attracting crowds of thousands wherever He went. Hearing reports of this, Prakāśānanda Sarasvatī, the leader of the prevailing Māyāvāda sect, began to criticize the Lord. A real spiritual leader, he said, would never involve himself in singing and dancing with all kinds of ordinary people. Ignorant of the spiritual significance of chanting the Hare Kṛṣṇa mantra, he considered it mere sentiment. Prakāśānanda Sarasvatī believed a spiritualist should continually study abstract philosophy and engage in lengthy discussions about the Absolute Truth. A great clash between a popular nonsectarian universal religious movement and a stifling separatist philosophy was about to occur. Śrī Caitanya Mahāprabhu would soon destroy forever the impersonalists' attempted domination over Indian spiritual thought and practice.

The Lord's followers were extremely unhappy about the Māyāvādīs' constant criticism of Him, so in order to pacify them He accepted an invitation to a meeting of all the leading Māyāvādīs. After seating Himself on the ground at the assembly, the Lord, exhibiting His supreme mystic potency, manifested from His body a spiritual effulgence more brilliant than the sun. The Māyāvādīs were amazed and immediately stood in respect. Then Prakāśānanda Sarasvatī inquired about why Śrī Caitanya chanted and danced instead of studying Vedānta philosophy. Lord Caitanya, who in truth was extremely well versed in the Vedic teachings, replied, "I have taken to the *saṅkīrtana* movement instead of the study of Vedānta because I am a great fool."

Indirectly, the Lord was criticizing the Māyāvādīs for being overly proud of their dry, intellectual study of the *Vedas,* which had led them to false conclusions. "And because I am a great fool," Caitanya continued, "my spiritual master forbade Me to play with Vedānta philosophy. He said that it is better that I chant the holy name of the Lord, for this would deliver Me from bondage." Śrī Caitanya then spoke a Sanskrit verse His spiritual master had told Him to always remember:

harer nāma harer nāma harer nāmaiva kevalam
kalau nāsty eva nāsty eva nāsty eva gatir anyathā

"In this age of Kali, there is no alternative, there is no alternative, there is no alternative for spiritual progress other than the chanting of the holy name, the chanting of the holy name, the chanting of the holy name of the Lord." (*Bṛhan-nāradīya Purāṇa*)

The discussion went on for hours. Finally, in one of the most astounding religious conversions of all time, Prakāśānanda Sarasvatī, the Māyāvādīs' greatest scholar, along with all his followers, surrendered to Lord Caitanya and began to chant the holy names of Kṛṣṇa with great enthusiasm. As a result of this conversion, the entire city of Benares adopted Śrī Caitanya's *saṅkīrtana* movement.

Although Śrī Caitanya had been born a *brāhmaṇa*, a member of the highest caste, He always said that such designations were external and behaved accordingly. Disregarding the social conventions of the age, He would stay in the homes of devotees from even the lowest caste and take His meals with them. Indeed, He delivered His most esoteric teachings on the subject of love of God to Rāmānanda Rāya, a member of a lower caste. Another of the Lord's disciples, Haridāsa Ṭhākura, was born a Muslim and was thus considered an outcast in Hindu society. Yet Śrī Caitanya elevated him to the exalted position of *nāmācārya*, the exemplar of the chanting of the holy name of Kṛṣṇa. Śrī Caitanya judged people not by their social status but by their spiritual advancement.

In this way, Lord Caitanya Mahāprabhu laid the foundation for a universal religion for all humankind – a scientific process of spiritual awakening that is now rapidly spreading around the globe. In this present age, when attendance at churches, temples, and mosques is diminishing daily and the world is torn by violence between numerous religious and political sects, it is easy to see that people are growing more and more dissatisfied with external, divisive religious formulas.

People are hungering for an experience of spirituality that transcends all boundaries. Millions are now finding that experience in the worldwide *saṅkīrtana* movement of Lord Caitanya, who said, "This *saṅkīrtana* movement is the prime benediction for humanity at large because it spreads the rays of the benediction moon. It is the life of all transcendental knowledge. It increases the ocean of transcendental bliss, and it enables us to fully taste the nectar for which we are always anxious."

CHAPTER SIX

Haridāsa Ṭhākura and the Prostitute

Strict followers of the caste system in sixteenth-century India avoided all contact with Muslims. Yet Śrī Caitanya Mahāprabhu, founder of the modern-day Hare Kṛṣṇa movement, shattered all bonds of prejudice and bigotry by elevating Haridāsa Ṭhākura, who was born in a Muslim family, to the position of nāmācārya, *or the exemplar of the holy name of Kṛṣṇa. In this way Śrī Caitanya practically demonstrated one of His central teachings: If any person is seen to be a great devotee of the Lord, he should be honored and respected regardless of his birth or social status. Such a spiritually advanced person can completely transform the lives of others. In the following incident from the life of Haridāsa Ṭhākura, we see how a beautiful prostitute became a great saint through the power of his chanting.*

In the forest of Benāpola, in what is now known as Bangladesh, the solitary monk sat before the sacred *tulasī* plant chanting the holy names of Kṛṣṇa day and night. Haridāsa Ṭhākura would chant three hundred thousand names of God each day. The body of this extraordinary saint, who was constantly in trance, was maintained by spiritual strength from chanting, and he barely slept at all. He was so influential that all the neighboring people offered their respects to him.

But a landholder named Rāmacandra Khān, the district tax collector, was envious of devotees of Lord Kṛṣṇa. Unable to tolerate the great respect that was being offered to Haridāsa Ṭhākura, he schemed to dishonor him. By no means, however, could he find any fault in Haridāsa's character. Therefore, he called for some local prostitutes and plotted with them to discredit the saint. Rāmacandra Khān said, "There is a mendicant named Haridāsa Ṭhākura. All of you devise a way to deviate him from his vows of austerity." Austerity means renunciation of sensual pleasures, especially the pleasure of sex.

Rāmacandra Khān selected a ravishing young beauty to break the monk's vow of celibacy and dishonor him. "I shall attract the mind of Haridāsa Ṭhākura within three days," she promised.

Rāmacandra Khān said to the prostitute, "My constable will go with you so that as soon as he sees you with Haridāsa Ṭhākura, he will immediately arrest him and bring both of you to me."

The prostitute replied, "First let me unite with him once; then the second time I shall take your constable with me to arrest him."

At night the prostitute, after dressing herself seductively, went to Haridāsa's cottage. Haridāsa was young, strong, and handsome, and the girl was eager to be alone with him. After offering respects to the *tulasī* plant, she went to the door of Haridāsa's hut, offered him obeisances, and stood there. Exposing part of her body to his view, she sat down on the threshold and spoke to him in sweet words.

"My dear Haridāsa, O great preacher, great devotee, you are so beautifully built and your youth is just beginning. What woman could control her mind after seeing you? I am eager to unite with you. My mind is greedy for this. If I don't obtain you, I shall not be able to keep body and soul together."

Haridāsa Ṭhākura replied, "I shall accept you without fail, but you will have to wait until I've finished chanting my regular rounds on my beads. Until that time, please sit and listen to the chanting of the holy name. As soon as I am finished, I shall fulfill your desire."

Hearing this, the prostitute remained sitting there while Haridāsa Ṭhākura chanted on his beads until the light of morning appeared. When she saw that it was morning, the prostitute stood up and left. Coming before Rāmacandra Khān she informed him of all the news.

"Today Haridāsa Ṭhākura has promised to enjoy with me," she said. "Tomorrow I shall certainly have union with him."

The next night, when the prostitute returned, Haridāsa Ṭhākura gave her many assurances. "Last night you were disappointed. Please excuse my offense. I shall certainly accept you. Please sit down and hear the chanting of the Hare Kṛṣṇa *mahā-mantra* until my regular chanting is finished. Then your desire will surely be fulfilled."

After offering her obeisances to the *tulasī* plant and Haridāsa Ṭhākura, she again sat down at the door. Hearing Haridāsa Ṭhākura chanting the Hare Kṛṣṇa mantra, she also chanted, "O my Lord Hari, O my Lord Hari."

When the night came to an end, the prostitute was restless. Seeing this, Haridāsa said, "I have vowed to chant ten million names in one month. I have taken this vow, but now it is nearing its end. I thought that today I would be able to finish my chanting of the Hare Kṛṣṇa mantra. I tried my best to chant the holy name all night, but I still did not finish. Tomorrow I will surely finish, and my vow will be fulfilled. Then it will be possible for me to enjoy with you in full freedom."

The prostitute returned to Rāmacandra Khān and informed him of what had happened. The next day she came earlier, at the beginning of the evening, and stayed all night. Again, as she began to hear Haridāsa Ṭhākura's chanting, she also chanted "Hari, Hari," the holy name of the Lord.

"Today it will be possible for me to finish my chanting," the saint said. "Then I shall satisfy all your desires."

The night ended with Haridāsa still chanting, but now, because of her constant hearing of Haridāsa's chanting, the prostitute's mind had changed. Now fully purified, she began to cry and fell at the feet of Haridāsa Ṭhākura, confessing that Rāmacandra Khān had appointed her to pollute him.

"Because I have taken the profession of a prostitute," she said, "I have performed unlimited sinful acts. My lord, be merciful to me. Deliver my fallen soul."

Haridāsa replied, "I know everything about Rāmacandra Khān's conspiracy. He is nothing but an ignorant fool, so his activities do not disturb me. On the very day Rāmacandra Khān was planning his intrigue against me I would have left this place, but because you came I stayed for three more days just to deliver you."

"Kindly act as my spiritual master," she begged him. "Instruct me in my duty so that I can get relief from this material existence."

Haridāsa answered, "Immediately go home and distribute to the *brāhmaṇas* whatever property you have. Then come back to this room and stay here forever in Kṛṣṇa consciousness. Chant the Hare Kṛṣṇa mantra continuously and render service to the *tulasī* plant by watering her and offering prayers to her. In this way you will very soon get the opportunity to be sheltered at the lotus feet of Kṛṣṇa."

After thus instructing the prostitute in the chanting of

Hare Kṛṣṇa, Haridāsa Ṭhākura stood up and left, continuously chanting the Kṛṣṇa's holy names.

Following the order of her spiritual master, the prostitute distributed to the local priests whatever household possessions she had. Following Haridāsa's example she began chanting the holy name of Kṛṣṇa three hundred thousand times a day. She chanted throughout the entire day and night, and she worshiped the *tulasī* plant. By sometimes eating frugally and at other times fasting, she conquered her senses. As soon as her senses were controlled, symptoms of love of God appeared in her person.

Thus the prostitute became a great saint, and her fame spread throughout the land. Because she was advanced in spiritual life, many devotees of the Lord came to see her. Seeing the sublime character of this former prostitute, everyone was astonished. They glorified the influence of Haridāsa Ṭhākura and offered their obeisances to him.

As for Rāmacandra Khān, he was eventually ruined, by the Lord's arrangement. Meanwhile, Haridāsa Ṭhākura continued his travels, always preaching the glories of the holy name, about which he often said, "As the rising sun immediately dissipates all the world's darkness, which is deep like an ocean, so the holy name of the Lord, if chanted once without offenses, can dissipate all the reactions of a living being's sinful life. All glories to that holy name of the Lord, which is auspicious for the entire world."

To this day thousands of pilgrims each year visit the tomb of Haridāsa Ṭhākura, who, although born a Muslim, became the exemplar of the chanting of the holy name and one of India's greatest devotee-saints.

CHAPTER SEVEN

The Science of Mantra Meditation

Excerpts from the writings of His Divine Grace
A. C. Bhaktivedanta Swami Prabhupāda

Reviving Our Original Brilliance

Sparks are beautiful as long as they are in the fire. Similarly, we have to remain in the association of the Supreme Personality of Godhead and always engage in devotional service, for then we shall always be brilliant and illuminating. As soon as we fall from the service of the Lord, our brilliance and illumination will immediately be extinguished, or at least stopped for some time. When we living entities, who are like sparks of the original fire, the Supreme Lord, fall into a material condition, we must take the mantra from the Supreme Personality of Godhead as it is offered by Śrī Caitanya Mahāprabhu. By chanting this Hare Kṛṣṇa mantra, we shall be delivered from all the difficulties of this material world.

Śrīmad-Bhāgavatam 8.6.15

The Mantra for Everyone

Caitanya Mahāprabhu introduced the chanting of Hare Kṛṣṇa, Hare Kṛṣṇa, Kṛṣṇa Kṛṣṇa, Hare Hare/ Hare Rāma, Hare Rāma, Rāma Rāma, Hare Hare as a great means of propaganda for spreading love of God. It is not that it is recommended only for Kali-yuga. Actually, it is recommended for every age. There have always been many devotees who have chanted and reached perfection in all ages. That is the beauty of this Kṛṣṇa consciousness movement. It is not simply for one age, or for one country, or for one class of people. Hare Kṛṣṇa can be chanted by anyone in any social position, in any country and in any age, for Kṛṣṇa is the Supreme Lord of all people in all social positions, in all countries, in all ages.

Elevation to Kṛṣṇa Consciousness

Awakening Our Original Consciousness

It is said in the *Caitanya-caritāmṛta,* "Pure love for Śrī Kṛṣṇa is eternally established in the hearts of living entities. It is not something to be gained from another source. When the heart is purified by hearing and chanting, the living entity naturally awakens." Since Kṛṣṇa consciousness is inherent in every living entity, everyone should be given a chance to hear about Śrī Kṛṣṇa. Simply by hearing and chanting – *śravaṇam kīrtanam* – one's heart is directly purified and one's original Kṛṣṇa consciousness is immediately awakened. Kṛṣṇa consciousness is not artificially imposed upon the heart; it is already there. When one chants the holy name of the Supreme Personality of Godhead, the heart is cleansed of all material contamination.

The Nectar of Instruction, Text 4

Chanting: The Universal Religion

In this present age quarrels take place even over trifles, and therefore the *śāstras* [scriptures] have recommended for this age a common platform for realization, namely chanting the holy names of the Lord. People can hold meetings to glorify the Lord in their respective languages and with melodious songs, and if such performances are executed in an offenseless manner, it is certain that the participants will gradually attain spiritual perfection without having to undergo more rigorous methods.... all people of the world will accept the holy name of the Lord as the common platform for the universal religion of mankind.

Śrīmad-Bhāgavatam, Canto One, Introduction

Seeing God Through Sound

Hare Kṛṣṇa, Hare Kṛṣṇa, Kṛṣṇa Kṛṣṇa, Hare Hare/ Hare Rāma, Hare Rāma, Rāma Rāma, Hare Hare is a sound (*śabda*) that is nondifferent from Kṛṣṇa. The sound Kṛṣṇa and the original Kṛṣṇa are the same....

There are things which we hear but do not see – the wind may be whistling past our ears, and we can hear it, but there is no possibility of seeing the wind. Since hearing is no less an important experience or valid one than seeing, we can hear Kṛṣṇa and realize His presence through sound. Śrī Kṛṣṇa Himself says, "I am not there in My abode or in the heart of the meditating yogi but where My pure devotees are singing." We can feel the presence of Kṛṣṇa as we actually make progress.

Rāja-vidyā: The King of Knowledge

The Holy Name Acts Like Fire

Fire will act, regardless of whether handled by an innocent child or by someone well aware of its power. For example, if a field of straw or dry grass is set afire, either by an elderly man who knows the power of fire or by a child who does not, the grass will be burned to ashes. Similarly, one may or may not know the power of chanting the Hare Kṛṣṇa mantra, but if one chants the holy name he will become free from all sinful reactions.

Śrīmad-Bhāgavatam 6.2.18

Liberation from False Ego

The effect of chanting the holy name of the Lord is perceived by the chanter as liberation from the conception of false egoism. False egoism is exhibited by thinking oneself to be the enjoyer of the world and thinking everything in the world to be meant for the enjoyment of one's self only. The whole materialistic world is moving under such false egoism of "I" and "mine," but the factual effect of chanting the holy name is to become free from such misconceptions.

Śrīmad-Bhāgavatam 2.1.11

Chanting Defeats Death

By the grace of the Lord, if a devotee, at the time of death, can simply chant His holy names – Hare Kṛṣṇa, Hare Kṛṣṇa, Kṛṣṇa Kṛṣṇa, Hare Hare/ Hare Rāma, Hare Rāma, Rāma Rāma, Hare Hare – simply by chanting this *mahā-mantra,* he immediately surpasses the great ocean of the material sky and enters the spiritual sky. He never has to come back for repetition of birth and death. Simply by chanting the holy name of the Lord, one can surpass the ocean of death.

Śrīmad-Bhāgavatam 4.10.30

Experiencing Ecstasy

The transcendental ecstatic attachment for Kṛṣṇa which results from perfectly understanding that Kṛṣṇa's person and name are identical is called *bhāva* [ecstatic spiritual emotion]. One who has attained *bhāva* is certainly not contaminated by material nature. He actually enjoys transcendental pleasure from *bhāva,* and when *bhāva* is intensified, it is called love of Godhead. Lord Caitanya taught that the holy name of Kṛṣṇa, called the *mahā-mantra* (great chanting), enables anyone who chants it to attain the stage of love of Godhead, or intensified *bhāva.*

Teachings of Lord Caitanya

The Sound Incarnation of God

Sometimes Kṛṣṇa descends personally, and sometimes He descends as sound vibration, and sometimes He descends as a devotee. There are many different categories of *avatāras.* In this present age Kṛṣṇa has descended in His holy name, Hare Kṛṣṇa, Hare Kṛṣṇa, Kṛṣṇa Kṛṣṇa, Hare Hare/ Hare Rāma, Hare Rāma, Rāma Rāma, Hare Hare. Lord Caitanya Mahāprabhu also confirmed that in this Age of Kali, Kṛṣṇa has descended in the form of sound vibration. Sound is one of the forms which the Lord takes. Therefore it is stated that there is no difference between Kṛṣṇa and His name.

Elevation to Kṛṣṇa Consciousness

Christ or Kṛṣṇa – the Name Is the Same

From a conversation with a Benedictine monk

Christos is the Greek version of the word *Kṛṣṇa.* When an Indian person calls on Kṛṣṇa, he often says, "Kṛṣṭa." *Kṛṣṭa* is a Sanskrit word meaning "attraction." So when we address God as "Christ," "Kṛṣṭa," or "Kṛṣṇa," we indicate the same all-attractive Supreme Personality of Godhead.

When Jesus said, "Our Father, who art in heaven, sanctified be Thy name," that name of God was "Kṛṣṭa" or "Kṛṣṇa." Actually it doesn't matter – Kṛṣṇa or Christ – the name is the same. The main point is to follow the injunctions of the Vedic scriptures that recommend chanting the name of God in this age. I have not come to teach you, but only to request you to please chant the name of God. The Bible also demands this of you. So let us kindly cooperate and chant, and if you have a prejudice against chanting the name Kṛṣṇa, then chant "Christos" or "Kṛṣṭa" – there is no difference.

Śrī Caitanya said, *nāmnām akāri bahudhā nija-sarva-śaktiḥ:* "God has millions and millions of names, and because there is no difference between God's name and Himself, each one of these names has the same potency as God." Therefore, even if you accept designations like "Hindu," "Christian," or "Muslim," if you simply chant the name of God found in your own scriptures you will attain the spiritual platform. We always have these beads, just as you have your rosary. You are chanting, but why don't the other Christians also chant? If you would like to cooperate with us, then go to the churches and chant, "Christ," "Kṛṣṭa," or "Kṛṣṇa." What could be the objection?

The Science of Self-Realization

The Wild Horses of the Mind

The mind is always concocting objects for happiness. I am always thinking, "This will make me happy" or "That will make me happy." "Happiness is here." "Happiness is there." In this way the mind is taking us anywhere and everywhere. It is as though we are riding on a chariot behind an unbridled horse. We have no power over where we are going but can only sit in horror and watch helplessly. As soon as the mind is engaged in the Kṛṣṇa consciousness process – specifically chanting Hare Kṛṣṇa, Hare Kṛṣṇa,

Kṛṣṇa Kṛṣṇa, Hare Hare/ Hare Rāma, Hare Rāma, Rāma Rāma, Hare Hare – then the wild horses of the mind will gradually come under our control.

On the Way to Kṛṣṇa

The Peace Formula

The earth is the property of God, but we, the living entities, especially the so-called civilized human beings, are claiming God's property as our own, under both an individual and collective false conception. If you want peace, you have to remove this false conception from your mind and from the world. This false claim of proprietorship by the human race on earth is partly or wholly the cause of all disturbances of peace on earth.

Foolish and so-called civilized men are claiming proprietary rights on the property of God because they have now become godless. You cannot be happy and peaceful in a godless society. In the *Bhagavad-gītā* Lord Kṛṣṇa says that He is the factual enjoyer of all activities of the living entities, that He is the Supreme Lord of all universes, and that He is the well-wishing friend of all beings. When the people of the world know this as the formula for peace, it is then and there that peace will prevail.

Therefore, if you want peace at all, you will have to change your consciousness into Kṛṣṇa consciousness, both individually and collectively, by the simple process of chanting the holy name of God. This is a standard and recognized process for achieving peace in the world. We therefore recommend that everyone become Kṛṣṇa conscious by chanting Hare Kṛṣṇa, Hare Kṛṣṇa, Kṛṣṇa Kṛṣṇa, Hare Hare/ Hare Rāma, Hare Rāma, Rāma Rāma, Hare Hare.

This is practical, simple, and sublime. Four hundred and eighty years ago this formula was introduced in India by Lord Śrī Caitanya, and now it is available in your country. Take to this simple process of chanting as above mentioned, realize your factual position by reading the *Bhagavad-gītā As It Is,* and reestablish your lost relationship with Kṛṣṇa, God. Peace and prosperity will be the immediate worldwide result.

The Science of Self-Realization

Free vs. High-priced Mantras

Recently, an Indian yogi came to America to give some "private mantra." But if a mantra has any power, why should it be private? If a mantra is powerful, why should it not be publicly declared so that everyone can take advantage of it? We are saying that this Hare Kṛṣṇa *mahā-mantra* can save everyone, and we are therefore distributing it publicly, free of charge.... The devotees are preaching without charge, declaring in the streets, parks, and everywhere, "Here! Here is the Hare Kṛṣṇa *mahā-mantra.* Come on, take it!"

The Path of Perfection

Rx for Heart Disease

From a conversation with a community relations officer with the Chicago police department

Lieutenant Mozee: Would there be more of a beneficial influence – more of a strengthening of the community – if the program [congregational chanting] were held in a poorer area rather than an affluent area?

Śrīla Prabhupāda: Our treatment is for the spiritually diseased person. When a person is afflicted with a disease, there are no distinctions between a poor man and a rich man. They are both admitted to the same hospital. Just as the hospital should be in a place where both the poor man and the rich man can easily come, the location of the *saṅkīrtana* facility should be easily accessible to all. Since everyone is materially infected, everyone should be able to take advantage.

So our chanting process is for everyone, because it cleanses the heart, regardless of the man's opulence or poverty. The only way to permanently change the criminal habit is to change the heart of the criminal. As you well know, many thieves are arrested numerous times and put into jail. Although they know that if they commit theft they will go to jail, still they are forced to steal, because of their unclean hearts. Therefore without cleansing the heart of the criminal, you cannot stop crime simply by more stringent law enforcement. The thief and the murderer already know the law, yet they still commit violent crimes due to their unclean hearts. So our process is to cleanse the heart. Then all the troubles of this material world will be solved.

The Science of Self-Realization

CHAPTER EIGHT

The Benefits of Chanting

Dr. Daniel Goleman, PhD, former associate editor of Psychology Today *and author* of The Meditative Mind: The Varieties of Meditative Experience *and the bestseller* Emotional Intelligence, *after studying the meditation techniques of members of the Hare Kṛṣṇa movement, said, "I found the Hare Kṛṣṇa devotees to be well-integrated, friendly, and productive human beings. In a culture like ours, in which inner, spiritual development is almost totally neglected in favor of materialistic pursuits, we might have something to learn from their meditational practices."*

Everyone knows that a happy life requires good health. Proper diet, adequate exercise, and sufficient rest are necessary to keep our bodies strong and fit. If we neglect these demands, our bodies become weakened and resistance wanes. Made susceptible to infection, we eventually fall ill.

More important but less well known is the inner self's need for spiritual nourishment and attention. If we ignore our spiritual health requirements, we become overwhelmed by negative material tendencies like anxiety, hatred, loneliness, prejudice, greed, boredom, envy, and anger.

In order to counteract and prevent these subtle infections of the self, we should, as recommended in the Vedic literatures and in many other scriptures, incorporate into our lives a program of self-examination and steady inner growth based on spiritual strength and mindful thinking.

The transcendental potency necessary for developing complete psychological and spiritual fulfillment is already present within everyone. It must, however, be uncovered by a genuine spiritual process. Of all such authentic processes, India's timeless *Vedas* tell us that meditation on the Hare Kṛṣṇa mantra is the most powerful.

The initial result of chanting the Hare Kṛṣṇa mantra is summarized by Śrīla Prabhupāda in his commentary on the *Bhagavad-gītā:* "We have practical experience that any person who is chanting the holy names of Kṛṣṇa (Hare Kṛṣṇa, Hare Kṛṣṇa, Kṛṣṇa Kṛṣṇa, Hare Hare/ Hare Rāma, Hare Rāma, Rāma Rāma, Hare Hare) in course of time feels some transcendental pleasure and very quickly becomes purified of all material contamination."

In the preliminary stages of chanting, practitioners experience a clearing of consciousness, peace of mind, and relief from unwanted drives and habits. As they develop more realization by chanting, they perceive the original, spiritual existence of the self. According to the *Bhagavad-gītā,* this enlightened state "is characterized by one's ability to see the self by the pure mind and to relish and rejoice in the self."

And in the *Caitanya-caritāmṛta,* a multivolume work describing the life and teachings of Śrī Caitanya, founder of the modern-day Kṛṣṇa consciousness movement, the ultimate benefit of chanting is described. "The result of chanting is that one awakens his love for Kṛṣṇa and tastes transcendental bliss. Ultimately, one attains the association of Kṛṣṇa and engages in His devotional service, as if immersing himself in a great ocean of love."

So by chanting Hare Kṛṣṇa, one reaps innumerable benefits, culminating in Kṛṣṇa consciousness and love of God. We can realize the fruits of chanting by adopting the process of mantra meditation and applying it systematically. For clear understanding of the progressive effects of chanting, some of the more important benefits are discussed separately.

Peace of Mind

Initially, meditation focuses on controlling the mind, for in our normal condition we are slaves to any whimsical thoughts, desires, and appetites the mind may generate. We think of something and immediately we want to do it. But the *Bhagavad-gītā* tells us that the meditator must learn to control the mind: "For one who has conquered the mind, the mind is the best of friends; but for one who has failed to do so, the mind will remain the greatest enemy."

The materialistic mind attempts to enjoy by employing the senses to experience matter and material relationships. It is full of unlimited ideas for sense gratification, and being perpetually restless, it constantly flickers from one sense object to another. In doing so the mind vacillates between hankering for some material gain and lamenting some loss or frustration.

In the *Bhagavad-gītā* Kṛṣṇa explains, "One who is not in transcendental consciousness can have neither a controlled mind nor steady intelligence, without which there is no possibility of peace. And how can there be any happiness without peace?" By chanting the Hare Kṛṣṇa mantra, we can control the mind instead of letting it control us.

Mantra is a Sanskrit word. *Man* means "mind" and *tra* means "to deliver." Thus a mantra is a transcendental sound vibration with potency to liberate the mind from material conditioning.

In his commentary on *Śrīmad-Bhāgavatam,* Prabhupāda explains, "Our entanglement in material affairs has begun from material sound." Each day we hear material sounds from radio and television, from friends and relatives, and based on what we hear, we act. But as Śrīla Prabhupāda points out, "There is sound in the spiritual world also. If we approach that sound, then our spiritual life begins." When we control the mind by focusing it on the purely spiritual sound vibration of the Hare Kṛṣṇa mantra, the mind becomes calm. As "music has charms to soothe a savage breast," so the spiritual sound of the mantra soothes the restless mind. The Hare Kṛṣṇa mantra, being imbued with God's own supreme energies, has the power to subdue all kinds of mental disturbance. Just as a reservoir of water is transparent when not agitated, our mental perceptions become clear and pure when the mind is no longer agitated by the waves of material desires. The mind in its pure state, like a mirror cleansed of dust, will then reflect undistorted images of reality, allowing us to go beneath the surface and perceive the essential spiritual quality of all life's experiences.

Knowledge of the Self

The *Vedas* state that consciousness is a symptom of the soul. In its pure condition, the soul exists in the spiritual world; but when it falls down into contact with matter, the living being is covered by an illusion called false egoism. False ego bewilders the consciousness, causing us to identify with our material bodies. But we are not our material body. When we look at our hand or leg, we say, "This is my hand" or "This is my leg." The conscious self, the "I," is therefore the owner and observer of the body. Intellectually, this fact is easily understandable, and by the spiritual realization that results from chanting, this truth can be directly and continuously experienced.

When the living being identifies with the material body and loses awareness of his real, spiritual self, he inevitably fears death, old age, and disease. He fears loss of beauty, intelligence, and strength and experiences countless other anxieties and false emotions relating to the temporary body. But when we begin regularly chanting Hare Kṛṣṇa, we soon realize ourselves to be pure and changeless spirit souls, completely distinct from the material body. Because the mantra is a completely pure spiritual sound vibration, it has the power to restore our consciousness to its original, uncontaminated condition. At this point, we cease to be controlled by jealousy, bigotry, pride, envy, and hatred. As Lord Kṛṣṇa tells us in the *Bhagavad-gītā,* the soul is "unborn, eternal, ever-existing, and primeval." As our false bodily identification dissolves and we perceive our true transcendental existence, we automatically transcend all the fears and anxieties of material existence. We no longer think, "I am American," "I am Russian," "I am black," "I am white."

Attaining personal self-awareness also gives us the ability to see the spiritual nature of other living beings. When our natural, spiritual feelings are awakened, we experience the ultimate unity of all life. This is what it means to become a liberated person: by spiritual realization we become free of our animosity and envy toward other living things.

This higher vision is explained by Śrīla Prabhupāda in *Transcendental Teachings of Prahlāda Mahārāja.* "When a person becomes fully Kṛṣṇa conscious, he does not think, 'Here is a man, here is an animal, here is a cat, here is a dog, here is a worm.' He sees everyone as part and parcel of Kṛṣṇa. This is very nicely explained in the *Bhagavad-gītā:* 'One who is actually learned in Kṛṣṇa consciousness becomes a lover of the universe.' Unless one is situated on the Kṛṣṇa conscious platform, there is no question of universal brotherhood."

Real Happiness

Everyone is thirsting for true and lasting happiness. But because material pleasure is limited and temporary, it is compared to a tiny drop of moisture in the desert. It can give us no permanent relief because while material sensations and relationships may touch the body and mind, they lack the potency to satisfy the soul's spiritual desires. The chanting of Hare Kṛṣṇa provides complete satisfaction because it places us in direct contact with God and His spiritual pleasure potency. God is full of all bliss, and when we enter His association, we can also experience the same transcendental happiness.

In the Vedic literature there is an interesting account of how the pleasure of chanting far exceeds any material benefit. Once a poor *brāhmaṇa* priest worshiped the demigod Śiva for a material benediction. Śiva, however, advised him to approach the sage Sanātana Gosvāmī to obtain his heart's desire. On learning that Sanātana Gosvāmī had a mystical stone capable of producing gold, the poor *brāhmaṇa* asked if he could have it. Sanātana consented and told the *brāhmaṇa* he could take the stone from its place – in his garbage pile. The *brāhmaṇa* left feeling great joy, for he could now get as much gold as he desired simply by touching the stone to iron. But as he walked away he thought, "If a touchstone is the best gift, why would Sanātana Gosvāmī keep it in the garbage?"

He returned to Sanātana Gosvāmī to find out. Sanātana Gosvāmī informed him, "Actually, that touchstone is not the best gift. But are you prepared to take the best benediction from me?"

"Yes," the poor *brāhmaṇa* replied. "I have come to you for the best benediction." Sanātana Gosvāmī then told him to throw the touchstone in the nearby river and return. The *brāhmaṇa* did so, and when he came back, the saintly Sanātana initiated him into the chanting of the Hare Kṛṣṇa mantra, the sublime method for experiencing the highest spiritual pleasure.

Liberation from Karma

The law of karma means that for every material action performed, nature forces an equivalent reaction on the performer – or, as the Bible states, "As ye sow, so shall ye reap."

Material activities can be compared to seeds. Initially they are performed, or "planted," and over the course of time they gradually fructify, releasing their resultant reactions. Enmeshed in this web of actions and reactions we are forced to accept one material body after another to experience our karmic destiny. But freedom from karma is possible by sincere chanting of Kṛṣṇa's transcendental names. Since God's names are filled with transcendental energy, when the living being associates with the divine sound vibration, he is freed from the endless cycle of karma.

Just as seeds fried in a pan lose their potency to sprout, so karmic reactions are rendered impotent by the power of God's holy names. Śrī Kṛṣṇa is like the sun. The sun is so powerful that it can purify whatever comes into contact with it. If any object enters the sun globe it is immediately becomes fire. Similarly, when our consciousness contacts and becomes absorbed in the transcendental sound "Kṛṣṇa," Śrī Kṛṣṇa's internal energies purify us of all karmic reactions. In his commentary on *Śrīmad-Bhāgavatam* Śrīla Prabhupāda stresses, "The holy name is so spiritually potent that simply by chanting the holy name one can be freed from the reactions to all sinful activity."

Freedom from Reincarnation

The *Vedas* teach that the living entity, the soul, is eternal, but due to past activities and material desires, it perpetually accepts different material bodies. As long as we have material desires, nature, acting under God's direction, will award us one material body after another. This is called transmigration of the soul, or reincarnation. Actually, this changing of bodies is not surprising because even in this life we go through many bodies. We start with the body of an infant, then change the infant's body for a child's. Gradually, the body changes into an adult body, then an old man's or woman's body. Similarly, when our present body dies, we get a new one to go on and enjoy and suffer the results of our karma, cycling again and again.

Liberation from this cycle of *saṁsāra,* as it is called, or the endless wheel of birth and death, is possible if we free our consciousness from material desires. By chanting Hare Kṛṣṇa we revive the soul's natural spiritual desires as well as our awareness of our true identity. Just as it is the nature of the body to be attracted to sense gratification, so it is the nature of the soul to be attracted to God. Chanting awakens our original God consciousness and our desire to serve and associate with Him. By this simple change in consciousness we can transcend the cycle of reincarnation.

Śrīla Prabhupāda discusses this in his commentary on the *Bhagavad-gītā*. "One's thoughts during the course of one's life accumulate to influence one's thoughts at the moment of death, so this life creates one's next life.... If [in this life] one is transcendentally absorbed in Kṛṣṇa's service, then his next body will be transcendental (spiritual), not material. Therefore the chanting of Hare Kṛṣṇa, Hare Kṛṣṇa, Kṛṣṇa Kṛṣṇa, Hare Hare/ Hare Rāma, Hare Rāma, Rāma Rāma, Hare Hare is the best process for successfully changing one's state of being at the end of one's life."

The Ultimate Benefit – Love of God

The final goal – and the highest fruit of chanting – is complete God realization and pure love of God.

As our consciousness becomes increasingly purified, our steady spiritual advancement is reflected in our character and behavior. As the sun approaches the horizon it is preceded by increasing warmth and illumination. Similarly, as realization of Kṛṣṇa's holy name is revived in the heart, this increasing spiritual awareness manifests in all aspects of our personality. Ultimately, the eternal, loving relationship between God and the living being is revived. Before entering the material world, each soul had a unique spiritual relationship with God. This loving relationship is thousands of times greater and more intense than any love experienced in the material world. This is described in the *Caitanya-caritāmṛta:* "Pure love for Kṛṣṇa is eternally established in the heart of the living entities. It is not something to be gained from another source. When the heart is purified by hearing and chanting, this love naturally awakens."

In our eternal, constitutional position in the spiritual world we are able to associate with God directly, serving Him in a spiritual form just suitable for our mood of love and devotion. In this relationship of spiritual love, the pure devotee is absorbed in transcendental ecstasy. This state of ecstasy is described in *The Nectar of Devotion.* "At that time one's heart becomes illuminated like the sun. The sun is far above the planetary systems, and there is no possibility of its being covered by any kind of cloud. Similarly, when a devotee is purified like the sun, from his heart there is a diffusion of ecstatic love more glorious than the sunshine."

CHAPTER NINE

The Dawn of Hare Kṛṣṇa in Britain

Excerpts from *When the Sun Shines*

by Ranchor Prime

1968

A new musical called *Hair* was attracting record audiences in London. It had originated in New York off Broadway as a protest against the Vietnam War. It told the story of a hippie tribe's search for happiness and peace, ending with one of them being forced into the army and killed in Vietnam. Such stories were a reality for peace-loving young Americans, including a good number who aspired to be Hare Kṛṣṇa devotees. A high point in the musical was a choreographed version of the Hare Kṛṣṇa mantra performed by the whole cast. *Hair* was a sensation on both sides of the Atlantic and was popularizing the mantra. It was all make-believe – the hippies on stage were professional actors – but it expressed a real yearning that existed among young people for spiritual revolution and for the dawn of a new age – the Age of Aquarius.

The devotees chanted nightly to the crowds on the pavement outside the Shaftesbury Theatre, where *Hair* was showing. They were not actors; they were the real thing – dedicated to their search for truth and peace. One night the members of the cast invited them in to chant on stage.

The cast of *Hair* performed the Hare Kṛṣṇa chant each night, but they did so while naked. A cultural revolution was in progress. Its intention was to change people's consciousness. John Lennon had just written its anthem, his song "Revolution," in which he sang that, while people say they want to change the constitution, "You'd better free your mind instead."

In this time of self-discovery and spiritual adventure the Beatles were leaders of the revolution. If they became Kṛṣṇa conscious, others would surely follow.

Savile Row, December 1968

The Beatles were looking for new talent. They had been exploited by the corporate music world, so now, following the untimely death of Brian Epstein, they had started Apple Corps to support independent artistic expression. "Send us your ideas," they announced.

Taking them at their word the devotees launched a campaign to get the Beatles' attention. They sent them a gift each day for a week – a photo of the New York devotees, arms upraised and with smiling faces, and the invitation, "Come sing with us!"; the Prahlāda story and Yamunā's IT cover; then a walking clockwork apple with the Hare Kṛṣṇa mantra painted on it and a home-baked apple pie. The gifts got through with the help of an American girl working as George Harrison's secretary. Finally, hoping they had excited some curiosity, they delivered their demo tape of the *Brahma-saṁhitā* prayers and a photograph of themselves.

They had no way of knowing if their campaign had been fruitful, but the opportunity to find out came in early December when Śyāmasundara received an unexpected phone call.

"Hi, I'm at the airport with some friends. Can you come and get us?" It was Rock Scully from San Francisco. Years before, he and Śyāmasundara had shared a room as Fulbright scholars in Switzerland. Later in California, when Rock was managing the Grateful Dead, he had helped Śyāmasundara put on the Mantra-Rock Dance.

Śyāmasundara drove to the airport, and three hours later the aging Ford Popular rounded the corner into Betterton Street crammed with passengers and laden with two Harley-Davidson machines. The whole party trooped upstairs, and after removing their heavy leather boots, settled down to a hearty meal. The two Hells Angels – their friend from San Francisco, Sonny Barger, and his mate Frenchy – had come to pay a visit to George Harrison in response to the invitation they claimed he had given them the previous year in Haight-Ashbury. Rock Scully had organized the expedition and Ken Kesey had come along for the ride.

Gurudāsa had been friends with Kesey previous to meeting the devotees. As author of the cult novel *One Flew Over the Cuckoo's Nest* Kesey was a folk hero of sixties America. The two of them spent the evening discussing philosophy, while the other guests, having feasted, fell into a deep sleep on the floor. When they awoke it was evening and they wanted to explore the city. Kicking their Harley-Davidsons into life, they roared off into the night. A few days later Rock called Śyāmasundara again.

"We've got an appointment to meet George Harrison tomorrow. You can come too."

Bringing another apple pie, Śyāmasundara walked to Savile Row, home of Apple Records. Rock's party was already inside causing the peaceable Apple staff a good deal of apprehension. Śyāmasundara, whose name was not on the list, was having trouble persuading the doormen to let him in. Just then Yoko Ono arrived and recognized him from the Arts Lab.

"You must be a friend of George's," she said kindly. "Come in with me."

Once in the crowded foyer he delivered his pie to the receptionist, who promised to pass it on to George, then found somewhere to sit. The room was filled with the noisy visitors from California, so Śyāmasundara decided to stay quietly in a corner and chant on his beads. Word came that all four Beatles were in a meeting. Time passed, and then one by one, John, Paul, and Ringo emerged and hastened to the exit without acknowledging the visitors. The party became restless and some left. Finally, when the foyer was half empty, George appeared. He looked round the room, spotted Śyāmasundara, and came straight over to him.

"Where have you been?" he exclaimed.

George sat down beside Śyāmasundara. "I've been waiting ages to meet you. I've seen Kṛṣṇa people in America, but I couldn't just go up and talk to them. Then a friend gave me Bhaktivedanta Swami's record. I can't stop listening to his voice. I started chanting Hare Kṛṣṇa along with him. I've listened so many times I've worn the record out."

Śyāmasundara listened in amazement as George told him how he had not only learned the chant but had listened carefully to Prabhupāda's recorded explanation of Kṛṣṇa consciousness. He had even taught the mantra to John Lennon, and together they had chanted Hare Kṛṣṇa on a yacht in the Greek islands.

"We carried on until our jaws ached. As soon as we stopped chanting, it was like the lights went out. It was amazing."

Śyāmasundara asked if George had received any of their gifts.

"Oh, yeah, we got everything. And more than a year ago I got a letter from one of you guys in San Francisco. I'm sorry I didn't reply – there's been too much happening. I've just been waiting for the chance to meet you."

"Well, Kṛṣṇa seems to have arranged that," laughed Śyāmasundara.

"So where is Bhaktivedanta Swami now?"

"He's in Los Angeles, but he'll come to London soon."

"I feel like I already know him – I've heard his voice so much. I really want to meet him. And I want to talk more with you. Can you make it out to my place this Sunday afternoon? Then we can spend as much time as we like and we can chant together." George drew a map to his house, and after thanking Śyāmasundara for coming, saw him to the door.

Esher, Surrey, Sunday 8th December 1968

Śyāmasundara rang George's doorbell. He carried a parcel of savories and sweets specially prepared by Yamunā. George opened the door and invited him in. While George's wife Pattie took the delicacies to the kitchen, George led his guest into a spacious room decorated with paintings of Hindu deities: Śiva performing his cosmic dance, the benign elephant-headed Gaṇeśa, and Sarasvatī, goddess of the arts, holding her stringed vina. On the mantelpiece sat framed photos of George's yoga masters, Yogananda and Yukteswar, with incense burning before them, and a picture of Prabhupāda.

George was no stranger to the yoga path or to chanting mantras. Three years earlier he had met Ravi Shankar and gone to India to study sitar with him. Then he had met Maharishi, and for three months in early 1968 he had stayed at Maharishi's ashram in Rishikesh to learn mantra meditation. George had lots of questions, and Śyāmasundara did his best to answer them. George especially wanted to know more about Bhaktivedanta Swami.

"Śrīla Prabhupāda represents an unbroken line of

teachers that stretches back thousands of years," explained Śyāmasundara. "Although he is deeply learned and has written several books, he thinks of himself as everyone's servant. He always says that his qualification to be a guru is that he is teaching us exactly what he has heard from his own guru. He hasn't added anything or taken anything away. That's why we trust him." George listened.

"The essence of Kṛṣṇa consciousness is to love Kṛṣṇa. We do that by serving Kṛṣṇa in everything we do and by chanting Kṛṣṇa's names. Prabhupāda says the name of God and God himself are nondifferent. When you chant Kṛṣṇa's name Kṛṣṇa dances on your tongue."

"But how do you avoid being distracted by *māyā*?" George knew about *māyā,* the illusion of material life, and how hard it could be to follow the yoga path when you are surrounded by people intent on other goals.

"That's the power of chanting," Śyāmasundara replied, and he described how as long as you chanted Kṛṣṇa's name you were with Kṛṣṇa. Consequently *māyā* had no power over you. Prabhupāda had written all about this in his edition of the *Bhagavad-gītā,* he said. "It has just been published in New York, and soon we'll have copies here in London. I'll give you one."

"Yes, I'd like that very much," said George. "But why do you only chant to Kṛṣṇa? What about Śiva or Sarasvatī?"

"Our spiritual master says that Kṛṣṇa is the origin of all other forms of God. He is the original candle from whom all other candles have been lit: each candle has equal brightness, but the first candle is the source of all the others. So Kṛṣṇa includes all other deities – there is no need for us to chant to them separately. We depend on Kṛṣṇa for everything."

They talked for a long time, then began to chant together, George playing his Indian harmonium, Śyāmasundara keeping time with the *karatālas.* Pattie joined in. When the afternoon ended, George knew he had found someone he could talk to frankly and openly about his spiritual path. He became thoughtful. George wanted to meet and chant with the rest of the devotees, and he had developed a taste for their cooking. So it was agreed that in a week or two, as soon as he could get free, he would visit their temple in Covent Garden.

"See you soon, then," said Śyāmasundara as he climbed into his car. "Hare Kṛṣṇa!"

"Hare Kṛṣṇa!" answered George, waving goodbye. They each felt they had found a friend.

* * *

At George's home George showed the devotees his studio and introduced them to Billy Preston, a brilliant young keyboard player he had brought over from America. The devotees got out their instruments and settled down with a sense of anticipation for the main event – the *kīrtana*.

Billy Preston played the electric organ, George sat at his white upright harmonium to begin with, then picked up a bass guitar, Mukunda beat the *mṛdaṅga,* Colin played George's tablas, Śyāmasundara the *esaraj,* Gurudāsa the tambura, and Jānakī and Mālatī the *karatālas*. Yamunā sang the lead, at times calling *"Haribol*!" at the top of her lungs. They chanted for an hour or so, switched instruments, and chanted again. For three hours the chant went on – long, deep, and languorous. George had learned to love chanting by hearing Prabhupāda's album, and now that he had others to share the chanting with he didn't want to stop.

That night, after chanting together for hours, something changed. A deep connection was forged between them, a sense of spiritual community that transcended any differences they might have on the material plane. At the end, as the devotees were preparing to leave, George spoke the words that were on everyone's mind.

"We have to make a record."

This was what the devotees had longed for. Even back in San Francisco they had sometimes dreamed of what it would be like to record the Hare Kṛṣṇa mantra with the Beatles. Now, without artifice, the door was opening. It was more of Kṛṣṇa's magic.

As Colin left George came up to him. "I saw how much you enjoyed the tablas," he said. "They're yours, man. Look after them." And George handed him the drums.

A week later George came round to the temple. He had just been to Spain. "I wrote a song about you guys," he said. "It's called 'Here Comes the Sun.'" After that George became a regular visitor at the temple, and the devotees sometimes went to his home.

Heathrow Airport, September 11, 1969

A light drizzle fell from a gray sky as Prabhupāda descended the steps from the plane at Heathrow. He was met by an immigration official and a policeman, whose job it was to take him directly to the VIP lounge. From behind a barrier his disciples waved and called. With his escort Prabhupāda broke away from the huddle of disembarking passengers and came straight over to them.

Once in the VIP lounge they enthroned him before the waiting press, garlanded him, and sat at his feet. He was swathed in saffron and heaped with flowers. Prabhupāda began to chant, playing his *karatālas* and singing with abandon. When he finished, Mukunda stood and invited the reporters' questions.

"I am trying to teach what you have forgotten," began Prabhupāda, addressing the newsmen. These words, delivered with an urgency and conviction the reporters did not expect, opened his mission to the people of England. The press conference, organized with Apple's help, was his first face-to-face encounter on English soil with the people whose culture and ideas had dominated his childhood. He went straight to the heart of what he had to teach.

"Some of you are saying there is no God or that God is dead, and some of you are saying that God is impersonal or void. I want to teach that there *is* God. It is a challenge to the atheistic people. There *is* God."

The British Empire had dominated India for close to two hundred years, including the first fifty years of Prabhupāda's life. During that time the British had imposed their ideas on India; now he would not compromise in what he had to tell them.

"As we are sitting here face to face, similarly you can see God face to face if you are serious and sincere."

Around forty journalists had come to meet the Beatles' new guru. George Harrison had given the public something unexpected – a mantra, the "Hare Kṛṣṇa Mantra," released on the Apple label by a group calling themselves the Rādhā Kṛṣṇa Temple. Their chanting was so magical, so different, that it had captivated London. The reporters wanted to know what it was all about. Prabhupāda was there to tell them.

"Unfortunately we are trying to forget God. Therefore we are embracing so many miseries. I am simply teaching that you be Kṛṣṇa conscious and *be happy*. Don't be swayed away by the waves of illusion."

Two years earlier the Beatles had met Mahesh Yogi, known as the Maharishi. For a few months, Maharishi's long hair and beard, beatific smile, and armfuls of flowers had represented, in the eyes of the Western media, the archetypal image of an Indian guru. But Prabhupāda was a different kind of guru. He was no trendy swami; he was penetrating and intense, and he demanded to be taken seriously. One of the reporters spoke up.

"Sir, is this singing essential to the sustenance of your faith?"

"This singing is the process for clearing the dust

accumulated on the heart. Our relationship with God is eternal and cannot be broken. Due to contact with *māyā* we are trying to forget Him, but if we chant this holy name of God, Hare Kṛṣṇa, then *māyā* will not act and we shall very quickly understand our relationship with God."

He cited several Sanskrit verses that explained the qualifications one needed to become Kṛṣṇa conscious. But he was not here to convert the British to his religion; he was not concerned with such sectarian ideas. When a reporter asked about the fighting between Christian denominations in Ireland, which by 1969 had reached new levels of violence, Prabhupāda did not hesitate. "We are not Christians or Hindus or Muslims. We are God's servants. Among God's servants there is no disagreement. First-class religion teaches how to love God. It doesn't matter if it is Christian or Muslim or Hindu. If you are Christian and you have developed your sense of loving God, then you are perfect."

"These are not ordinary boys and girls," Prabhupāda then said, indicating his disciples. "They are very elevated. Their qualities are greater than any mundane scholar's. For anyone who has developed love of Kṛṣṇa, all good qualities will automatically arise in them. Let anyone come and test these people and you shall see."

Prabhupāda had good reason to be proud of his young followers, for they had succeeded in laying a foundation for Kṛṣṇa consciousness in Britain where, thirty-five years earlier, his seasoned godbrothers had failed. They had succeeded because they loved to sing Hare Kṛṣṇa and they loved their teacher and wanted to do whatever they could to please him. They were not driven by ambition; they simply wanted to make their teacher happy. That made *them* happy, and their happiness communicated itself to those around them.

Once the questions were over the devotees led Prabhupāda to the waiting Rolls Royce. The driver helped him into the car, and as they looked lovingly at Prabhupāda, who appeared so wonderful sitting alone in the back seat, the car glided away. Only then did they realize that no one had accompanied him. The car and driver had been sent by John Lennon. For nearly two weeks the devotees had been living at Tittenhurst and preparing for Prabhupāda's stay.

John Lennon had kept the devotees busy as soon as they had arrived at Tittenhurst. Slacking was not allowed. Their first job had been to assist John and Yoko to move in. Then they had begun to redecorate the main house. John had wanted it stripped of unnecessary furniture and carpeting and painted white. There was much to be done in the garden too.

Near the main house was the gallery, originally a music room, with a high ceiling and good acoustics. John let the devotees use this room as their temple for as long as they were at Tittenhurst.

In those first few days before Prabhupāda arrived they had started meeting in the new temple morning and evening for *kīrtana* and class. John and Yoko had attended a few times and sat at the back listening, with John occasionally joining in the chanting. Once, George had come down with Pattie, and he too had chanted with the devotees.

The chauffeur drove on in silence. From the spacious back seat of the car, Prabhupāda saw a green, undulating landscape, whose sandy soil supported woods of pine and oak, interspersed with fern and gorse, and patches of grass where wild deer grazed. After only a few miles they reached the gates of Tittenhurst Park.

During the nineteenth century Tittenhurst Park had belonged to the great philanthropist Thomas Holloway. Like Holloway, John Lennon wanted to leave his mark on the world – but by promoting peace and bringing about a revolution in consciousness. Yet although he was lavishing money on renovating Tittenhurst, he no longer felt comfortable in England. America was safer from reporters and lawyers. But the American government refused him a visa. So he and Yoko, with her six-year-old daughter, sought sanctuary at Tittenhurst instead. The place suited him for the same reason it suited his predecessors: it was secluded but within easy reach of London, and it was close to Heathrow Airport. It was somewhere he could retreat with his new family, entertain friends, compose and record his own music without corporate interference – and have time to think. A temporary refuge for a troubled genius.

Tittenhurst would also serve as a retreat for Prabhupāda; it was a place where he could live quietly for a few weeks with his disciples. The two contrasting figures, John and Prabhupāda, were both only passing through Tittenhurst, and though they would share its cedar groves they would hardly meet. John, when he was not away recording the Beatles' last album at Abbey Road or working on his solo music with Yoko, ranged through his mansion's empty rooms, while Prabhupāda lived quietly in the cottage or walked among the trees with his disciples in the early mornings.

Still, John was deeply intrigued by Prabhupāda. He had met Prabhupāda's disciples and engaged them in serious discussions enough times to know that Prabhupāda was a man to be taken seriously. He was not going to be like the Maharishi, whom John had found disappointing. John had a serious nature – he liked to ask penetrating questions and then to hear, carefully, what people had to say. After hearing he would make up his own mind about life and say what he thought without compromise.

Having watched Prabhupāda's car leave the airport the devotees scrambled into their Land Rover, borrowed from John, and set off in pursuit. They hoped to arrive ahead of Prabhupāda so they could show him to his quarters. But when they reached Tittenhurst they found him standing alone in the driveway with his luggage. The rain had stopped and he waited patiently.

"Where should I go?" he asked in a relaxed mood.

Gurudāsa led the way down the path to Prabhupāda's cottage, through an arched front door, and up bare wooden stairs to a suite of two small rooms. The front room was a bedroom that overlooked the entrance courtyard; in the rear, with its small adjoining bathroom, was a cozy square sitting room with a high ceiling and a view across the garden. Apart from a set of shelves for his books, a low table for his desk, a cushion for his seat, and a borrowed carpet, the room was empty. This was how he liked to live: simply, as a *sannyāsī*.

As soon as Prabhupāda's luggage was deposited in his rooms he wanted to see the temple room. The devotees went with him and crowded in.

"Yamunā? Come and lead a *kīrtana*."

Yamunā sat on the floor in the middle of the room with the harmonium and sang. It was a wonderful moment. For a full year Prabhupāda's emissaries had labored to serve him in London. Now, with their new British brothers and sisters gathered round them, they were reunited with their master in *kīrtana*. The chanting swelled and Prabhupāda smiled with pleasure. After half an hour he brought the *kīrtana* to a close and began to speak.

George Harrison had come down to Tittenhurst and had arranged with John that they would see Prabhupāda together. While Prabhupāda returned to his rooms, John and George joined the devotees for a late lunch. It was a moment of friendship and informality before the serious meeting that would follow.

When the meal was over, John, Yoko, and George made their way with Śyāmasundara down the path to Prabhupāda's cottage and into his small sitting room. Fortune had arranged this encounter, in this secluded spot amid the shifting landscapes of the late sixties, bringing two of the most influential young men of their generation together with Kṛṣṇa's personal envoy.

Prabhupāda smiled benevolently as his guests settled themselves and Śyāmasundara garlanded each of them. John and George sat facing Prabhupāda. John wanted a role in the world beyond being a musician, to make a difference, with his declarations for Revolution, for Love, Not War, and his challenges to the establishment. That was why he had asked Prabhupāda and the devotees to come and stay. He recognized them as comrades from whom he might learn, and he wanted to help them bring their change in their way. All this was apparent to Prabhupāda.

"By the grace of Kṛṣṇa you are leaders," he began, addressing John and George together. "Thousands of young men follow you. They like you. If you give them something nice, the face of the world will change."

Prabhupāda's voice was soft and amiable as he spoke of Kṛṣṇa as the universal father. "We are all Kṛṣṇa's children," he said, quoting the *Bhagavad-gītā*. "If we think of him, we chant Hare Kṛṣṇa, we will have everything to gain and nothing to lose. Chant Hare Kṛṣṇa, everyone. Dance in ecstasy. My request is that you try to understand this Kṛṣṇa consciousness philosophy and make your own judgement.

"You want peace – I have read your statements," he spoke directly to John. "But we must know the process. Kṛṣṇa says, 'I am the enjoyer, I am the owner, I am the friend.'" These were the words Prabhupāda always referred to as the "Peace Formula."

"Why do we claim 'This is mine?' Kṛṣṇa is the Lord of every place. We come here in the kingdom of God and we claim, 'This is my property.' Is it not insanity?" He smiled at John, and looked around him and out of the window at the beautiful gardens. John, whose claim to Tittenhurst was the obvious example, remained silent.

"Kṛṣṇa is the friend of everyone. He is such a nice friend that He is living with me in my heart. Therefore I think people should have one God, Kṛṣṇa; one scripture, the

Bhagavad-gītā; one mantra, Hare Kṛṣṇa; and one activity, to serve Kṛṣṇa. Then there will be peace all over the world."

Had John read his edition of *Bhagavad-gītā*, Prabhupāda asked. John murmured that he had dipped into the *Gītā* during his three-month stay at Maharishi's ashram in Rishikesh but had not read Prabhupāda's commentary.

"We want people to be happy," continued Prabhupāda. "Be happy and make all others happy – that is Kṛṣṇa consciousness. But here in the material world you cannot be happy because everything is temporary."

This was something John could understand. He had achieved immense success, but he was at odds with the world and tortured by drug addiction. Prabhupāda's words were self-evident, and John listened closely as he explained that the soul, which is eternal, cannot find happiness in a temporary world. The solution, Prabhupāda said, was to go to the eternal world to be with Kṛṣṇa.

Understanding that his guests were musicians, Prabhupāda wanted them to hear Vedic mantras, so he chanted some verses from the *Śrīmad-Bhāgavatam*. His voice filled the room with deep and melodious tones. The verses said that people addicted to material life, to "chewing the already chewed," were not attracted to Kṛṣṇa. They were like the blind following the blind, misled and bound by miseries, and their only hope of freedom was to find the shelter of a pure devotee of God.

"You don't have to understand the words," he assured them. "Just hear the sound vibration and it will benefit you. All Sanskrit verses – for example, the verses of the *Bhagavad-gītā* – are mantras that can be sung like this." He encouraged them to use such verses to create sacred music.

CHAPTER TEN

Techniques for Chanting

The meditation business is flourishing these days. Modern-day "messiahs," "gurus," and "incarnations," carrying all kinds of mantras, are a dime a dozen, as eager customers flock to the feet of self-styled saviors. One so-called guru instructs his disciples in supercharged techniques for becoming a financial success. Another tells his followers that meditation will make their intelligence sharper and the body more fit to enjoy sensual pleasures. Still other "gurus" claim that sex is the ultimate goal of life and that unlimited sex will free one from all material desires. Some chic spiritual seekers pay a lot of money for secret mantras that they believe will allow them to perform mystic feats. But the Vedic literatures issue stern warnings about charlatan gurus and bogus mantras.

If a person is actually serious about spiritual life, he or she must come in contact with a bona fide spiritual master and learn from that person the science of Kṛṣṇa consciousness. The *Muṇḍaka Upaniṣad* states that "In order to learn the transcendental science, one must approach the bona fide spiritual master in disciplic succession, who is fixed in the Absolute Truth."

Not just any guru will do. This verse informs us that the spiritual master must be in disciplic succession from Lord Kṛṣṇa, the supreme spiritual master. Such genuine spiritual masters receive Kṛṣṇa's teachings through the disciplic chain and distribute them exactly as they have heard them from their spiritual master, without watering them down or altering them to suit their own whims. Bona fide gurus are not impersonalists or voidists and will never claim to be God; rather, they aspire to be a servant of God and His devotees. Such gurus are *ācāryas,* those who teach by example. Their lives are free from all material desires and sinful behavior, their character is exemplary, and they must be qualified to deliver their disciples from the path of repeated birth and death. The Kṛṣṇa conscious guru is absorbed in service to and meditation on the Supreme Lord at every moment.

Since the holy name of Kṛṣṇa is completely spiritual, it must be received from a pure representative or servant of Kṛṣṇa, who acts as a transparent medium between God and the sincere spiritual seeker. Mantras received from any other type of "guru" simply will not work.

Śrīla Prabhupāda writes in his commentary on *Śrīmad-Bhāgavatam:* "Unless one follows the disciplic succession, the mantra one receives will be chanted for no purpose. Nowadays there are so many rascal gurus who manufacture their mantras as a process for material advancement, not for spiritual advancement. Still, the mantra cannot be successful if it is manufactured. Mantras and the process of devotional service have special power, provided they are received from the authorized person."

Receiving the Hare Kṛṣṇa mantra from a bona fide guru

who is in complete harmony with Kṛṣṇa's teachings in the *Bhagavad-gītā* is the single most important aspect of chanting Hare Kṛṣṇa.

Chanting the Hare Kṛṣṇa *mahā-mantra* is the simplest of all processes of self-realization. There are no exorbitant fees; the mantra is free. The thriving business of selling mantras is a form of cheating. The test of a person's sincerity is not that he pays some money but that he is willing to change his life.

In order to chant Hare Kṛṣṇa, one need not equip oneself with expensive props and paraphernalia, learn to stand on one's head, or perform difficult postures or breathing exercises. The only equipment one needs is a tongue and ears. Everyone already has these. The tongue simply has to vibrate Kṛṣṇa's holy names, and the ears must hear it. By this simple process alone, one can achieve all perfection.

How to Chant

There are no hard-and-fast rules for chanting Hare Kṛṣṇa. The most wonderful thing about mantra meditation is that one may chant anywhere – at home, at work, driving in the car, or riding on the bus or subway. And one may chant at any time.

There are two basic types of chanting. Personal meditation, where one chants alone on beads, is called *japa*. When one chants in responsive fashion with others, this is called *kīrtana*. *Kīrtana* is usually accompanied by musical instruments and clapping. Both forms of chanting are recommended and beneficial.

To perform the first type of meditation, one needs only a set of *japa* beads. These may be purchased from any Hare Kṛṣṇa temple. Or, if you like, you can make your own beads at home.

If you decide to make your *japa* beads, follow these simple instructions:

1. Buy 109 large round beads (at least as big as a dime), and some strong, thick nylon thread.

2. Tie a knot about six inches from the end of a long piece of the thread and then string the beads, tying a knot after each one.

3. After stringing 108 beads, pull the two ends of thread through one large master bead.

4. This bead is called the Kṛṣṇa bead. Tie a knot next to it and cut off the excess thread. You now have your own set of *japa* beads.

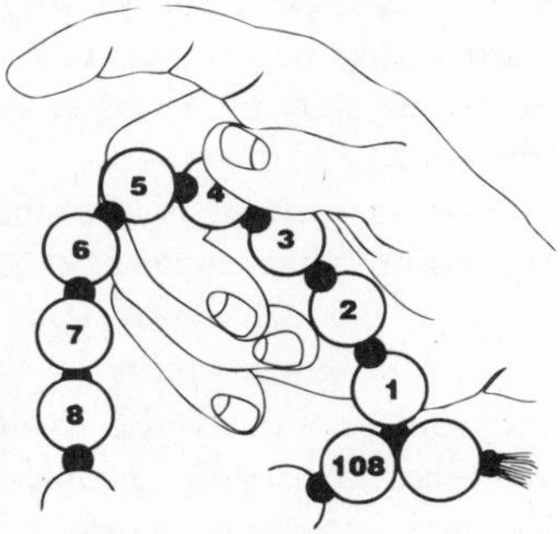

To meditate with the beads, hold them in your right hand. Gently roll the first bead between your thumb and middle finger as you chant the complete *mahā-mantra* – Hare Kṛṣṇa, Hare Kṛṣṇa, Kṛṣṇa Kṛṣṇa, Hare Hare/ Hare Rāma, Hare Rāma, Rāma Rāma, Hare Hare. Then go to the next bead, rolling it between the same two fingers while again chanting the entire mantra. Then go on to the next bead and then the next, continuing in this way until you have chanted on all 108 beads and have come to the Kṛṣṇa bead. You have now completed one round of chanting. Do not chant on the Kṛṣṇa bead, but turn the beads around and chant on them in the opposite direction, one after another. Chanting on beads is especially helpful because it engages the sense of touch during the meditative process and helps you concentrate even more on the sound of the mantra.

You may want to chant *japa* indoors, but you can chant just as comfortably walking along the beach or hiking in the mountains. Just bring your beads with you. If you chant sitting down, assume a comfortable position (preferably not lying down or slouching – sitting straight helps avoid the tendency to fall asleep). You can chant as loudly or as softly as you like, but it's important to pronounce the mantra clearly and loudly enough to hear yourself. The mind may have a tendency to wander off to other matters when you chant, for the mind is flickering and unsteady, always looking for something new and pleasurable to absorb itself in. If your mind wanders (to anything except Kṛṣṇa and things related to Him), gently bring it back to the transcendental sound vibration. It won't be difficult, because the mind is easily satisfied when absorbed in the divine sound of the Lord's holy names (unlike other meditational practices, where we may be asked to fix the mind on "nothing" or "the void").

One may chant *japa* at any time, but the Vedic literatures note that certain hours of the day are most auspicious for performing spiritual activities. The early morning hours just before and after sunrise are generally a time of stillness and quietude, excellently suited to contemplative chanting. Many people find it especially helpful to set aside a certain amount of time at the same time each day for chanting. Start with one or two rounds a day, and gradually increase the number until you reach sixteen, the recommended minimum for serious chanters.

While *japa* is a form of meditation involving you, your beads, and the Supreme Lord, *kīrtana,* on the other hand, is a form of group meditation in which one sings the mantra, sometimes accompanied by musical instruments. You may have seen a *kīrtana* party chanting on the streets of your city – Hare Kṛṣṇa devotees frequently perform this type of chanting to demonstrate the process and allow as many people as possible to benefit from hearing the holy names.

One may hold a *kīrtana* at home with family or friends, with one person leading the chanting and the others responding. *Kīrtana* is more of a supercharged meditational process, where in addition to hearing oneself chant one also benefits by hearing the chanting of others. Musical instruments are nice but not necessary. One may sing the mantra to any melody and clap his or her hands. (But if you are interested in the traditional melodies, ask at any Hare Kṛṣṇa temple.) If you have children, they can sing along as well and make spiritual advancement. You can get the whole family together every evening for chanting.

The sounds of the material world are boring, hackneyed, and monotonous, but chanting is an ever-increasingly refreshing experience. You can test this premise yourself. Try chanting some word or phrase for even five minutes. If you chant "Coca-Cola" over and over again, even for a few minutes, it becomes practically unbearable. There's no pleasure in it. But the sound of Kṛṣṇa's names is transcendental, and as we chant we want to chant more and more.

Enhancing Your Chanting

Although one receives immense benefit however and whenever one may chant Hare Kṛṣṇa, the great spiritual masters who are authorities on chanting suggest that a serious practitioner use certain practical techniques to enhance the chanting and bring quicker results.

The more we chant, the more easily we will be able to follow the yogic principles listed below, for as we chant we gain spiritual strength and develop a taste for higher, more spiritual forms of pleasure. When we begin to relish spiritual pleasure from chanting, giving up bad habits that may hinder our spiritual progress becomes much easier.

1. Just by chanting the Hare Kṛṣṇa mantra, one will automatically want to follow the four regulative principles of spiritual life:

   a. No eating of meat, fish, or eggs: to increase compassion, mercy, and nonviolence (*ahiṁsā*).
   b. No intoxicants: to achieve mental and physical

clarity and focus, and to develop the determination for spiritual practice.

c. No gambling: to increase truthfulness and to decrease anxiety, greed, envy, and anger.

d. No illicit sex (sex outside of marriage or not meant for the procreation of God conscious children): to decrease bodily identification and increase physical and mental cleanliness.

The four above-mentioned activities make it especially difficult for one to progress in spiritual life because they increase our attachment to material things. Therefore they are not recommended for those who wish to chant Hare Kṛṣṇa as a serious spiritual practice. The chanting is so powerful, however, that even if we are still involved with these things, we can still chant; the chanting will help us make the necessary adjustments.

2. One should regularly read the Vedic literatures, especially the *Bhagavad-gītā* and *Śrīmad-Bhāgavatam*. If one simply hears about God – His uncommon qualities and transcendental pastimes – the dust accumulated in the heart due to long association with the material world will be washed clean. By regularly hearing about Kṛṣṇa and the spiritual world, where Kṛṣṇa enjoys eternal pastimes with His devotees, one will fully understand the nature of the soul, true spiritual activities, and the complete procedure for obtaining release from the material world.

3. To be more fully immunized against material contamination, one should eat only vegetarian foods that have been spiritualized by offering them to God. There is a karmic reaction involved when one takes the life of any living being (including plants), but Kṛṣṇa states in the *Gītā* that if one offers Him vegetarian foods, He will nullify that reaction.

4. One should offer the fruit of one's work to God. When we work for our own pleasure or satisfaction, we must

accept the karmic reactions that come with our acts. If, however, we dedicate our work to God and work only for His satisfaction, there is no karmic reaction. Work performed as service to God not only frees us from karma but awakens our dormant love for Kṛṣṇa.

5. As much as possible, one who is serious about chanting Hare Kṛṣṇa should associate with like-minded persons. Like-minded friendships give great spiritual strength. Śrīla Prabhupāda formed the International Society for Krishna Consciousness so that persons who are sincere about becoming conscious of God and reviving their eternal loving relationship with Him may benefit from being with others on the same path back to the spiritual world.

Eventually, serious chanters will want to take initiation from a bona fide spiritual master. Initiation is recommended in the Vedic scriptures, for it dramatically helps one in chanting Hare Kṛṣṇa and assists in the awakening of our original spiritual consciousness. There are qualified spiritual masters in the International Society for Krishna Consciousness throughout the world who are willing to assist anyone sincerely wishing to become God conscious.

Śrīla Prabhupāda has indicated that those who desire to take initiation must follow the regulative principles mentioned earlier and chant each day on beads a minimum of sixteen rounds. Śrī Caitanya Mahāprabhu, the incarnation of Kṛṣṇa who popularized the chanting of the holy names five hundred years ago in India, introduced the system of chanting a fixed number of rounds each day. Careful completion of sixteen rounds daily will help the disciple to remember Kṛṣṇa always.

And that in essence is what Kṛṣṇa consciousness is all about – always remembering Kṛṣṇa and never forgetting Him. Chanting is the simplest way of maintaining this constant state of God consciousness, for the mystical potency contained in the mantra's vibration will always keep you in touch with God and your own original, spiritual nature.

All of God's innumerable spiritual potencies, including His transcendental pleasure principle, are contained in His holy names. Therefore the pleasure you will feel as you begin to chant will be far, far greater than any material happiness you have ever experienced. And the more you chant Hare Kṛṣṇa, the happier you will feel.

Sanskrit Pronunciation Guide

The system of transliteration used in this book conforms to a system that scholars have accepted to indicate the pronunciation of each sound in the Sanskrit language.

The short vowel **a** is pronounced like the **u** in b**u**t, long **ā** like the **a** in f**a**r. Short **i** is pronounced as in p**i**n, long **ī** as in p**i**que, short **u** as in p**u**ll, and long **ū** as in r**u**le. The vowel **ṛ** is pronounced like the **ri** in **ri**m, **e** like the **ey** in th**ey**, **o** like the **o** in g**o, ai** like the **ai** in **ai**sle, and **au** like the **ow** in h**ow**. The *anusvāra* (**ṁ**) is pronounced like the **n** in the French word *bo***n**, and *visarga* (**ḥ**) is pronounced as a final **h** sound. At the end of a couplet, **aḥ** is pronounced **aha**, and **iḥ** is pronounced **ihi**.

The guttural consonants – **k, kh, g, gh,** and **ṅ** – are pronounced from the throat in much the same manner as in English. **K** is pronounced as in **k**ite, **kh** as in Ec**kh**art, **g** as in **g**ive, **gh** as in di**g h**ard, and **ṅ** as in si**ng.**

The palatal consonants – **c, ch, j, jh,** and **ñ** – are pronounced with the tongue touching the firm ridge behind the teeth. **C** is pronounced as in **ch**air, **ch** as in staun**ch-h**eart, **j** as in **j**oy, **jh** as in he**dgeh**og, and **ñ** as in ca**ny**on.

The cerebral consonants – **ṭ, ṭh, ḍ, ḍh,** and **ṇ** – are pronounced with the tip of the tongue turned up and drawn back against the dome of the palate. **Ṭ** is pronounced as in **t**ub, **ṭh** as in ligh**t-h**eart, **ḍ** as in **d**ove, **ḍh** as in re**d-h**ot, and **ṇ** as in **n**ut. The dental consonants – **t, th, d, dh,** and **n** – are pronounced in the same manner as the cerebrals, but with the forepart of the tongue against the teeth.

The labial consonants – **p, ph, b, bh,** and **m** – are pronounced with the lips. **P** is pronounced as in **p**ine, **ph** as in u**ph**ill, **b** as in **b**ird, **bh** as in ru**b-h**ard, and **m** as in **m**other.

The semivowels – **y, r, l,** and **v** – are pronounced as in **y**es, **r**un, **l**ight, and **v**ine respectively. The sibilants – **ś, ṣ,** and **s** – are pronounced, respectively, as in the German word ***s****prechen* and the English words **sh**ine and **s**un. The letter **h** is pronounced as in **h**ome.

Centres of the International Society for Krishna Consciousness

For further information on classes, programmes, festivals, residential courses, and local meetings please contact the centre nearest you.

United Kingdom and Ireland

Belfast – Sri Sri Radha-Madhava Mandir, Brooklands, 140 Upper Dunmurray Lane, Belfast, BT17 0HE Tel: +44 (0)28 9062 0530; e-mail: belfast@iskcon.org.uk; www.iskconuk.com/belfast

Birmingham – 84 Stanmore Rd, Edgbaston, Birmingham, B16 9TB Tel: +44 (0)121 420 4999 e-mail: birmingham@iskcon.org.uk/ nitaicharan@fsmail.net; www.iskconbirmingham.org

Coventry – Radha Krishna Centre, Kingfield Rd, Coventry (mail: 19 Gloucester St, Coventry CV1 3BZ) Tel: +44 (0)2476 552822; e-mail: kov@krishnaofvrindavan.com; www.krishnaofvrindavan.com

Dublin – Govinda's Kirtan Centre, 83 Middle Abbey St, Dublin 1, Irish Republic Tel: +353 (0)87 992 1332; e-mail: syamananda@govindas.ie; www.govindas.ie

Leicester – 31 Granby Street, Leicester, LE1 6EP; Tel. +44 (0)116 276 2587/ +44(0)7597 786676 email: info@iskconleicester.org; www.iskconleicester.org

London (central) – Sri Sri Radha-Krishna Temple, 10 Soho St, London, W1D 3DL; Tel: +44 (0)20 7437 3662; Fax: +44 (0)20 7439 1127; e-mail: london@pamho.net; www.iskcon-london.org

London (Kings Cross) – Matchless Gifts, 102 Caledonian Road, Kings Cross, London N1 Tel: +44 (0)20 7168 5732; e-mail: foodforalluk@gmail.com; www.matchlessgifts.org.uk

London (south) – 42 Enmore Rd, South Norwood, London, SE25 5NG; Tel: +44 (0)20 8656 4296

Manchester – 20 Mayfield Rd, Whalley Range, Manchester, M16 8FT; Tel: +44 (0)161 226 4416 e-mail: contact@iskconmanchester.com; www.iskconmanchester.com

Swansea – The Hare Krishna Temple, 8 Craddock St, Swansea, SA1 3EN; Tel: +44 (0)1792 468469 e-mail: iskcon.swansea@pamho.net; www.iskconwales.org.uk

Newcastle-upon-Tyne – 304 Westgate Rd, Newcastle-upon-Tyne, NE4 6AR; Tel: +44 (0)191 272 2620; e-mail: newcastle@iskcon.org.uk; iskconnewcastle.wordpress.com

Scotland – Karuna Bhavan, Bankhouse Rd, Lesmahagow, Lanarkshire, ML11 0ES; Tel: +44 (0)1555 894790; Fax: +44 (0)1555 894526; e-mail: karuna.bhavan@aol.com; www.iskconuk.com/scotland

Watford – Bhaktivedanta Manor, Hilfield Lane, Watford, WD25 8EZ; Tel: +44 (0)1923 851000 Fax: +44 (0)1923 852896; e-mail: info@krishnatemple.com; www.krishnatemple.com

Rural Community

Upper Lough Erne (Northern Ireland) – Hare Krishna Temple, Krishna Island, Derrylin, Co. Fermanagh, BT92 9GN; Tel: +44 (0)28 677 21512; e-mail: secretary@krishnaisland.com; www.krishnaisland.com

Restaurants

Cardiff – Tel: +44 (0)2920 390391; e-mail: iskcon.wales@pamho.net; www.iskconwales.org.uk

Dublin - Govinda's, 4 Aungier St, Dublin 2, Irish Republic; Tel: +353 (0)1 475 0309 e-mail: nicola@govindas.ie; www.govindas.ie

Dublin – Govinda's, 83 Middle Abbey St, Dublin 1, Irish Republic e-mail: mark@govindas.ie; www.govindas.ie

Dublin – Govinda's, 18 Merrion Row, Dublin 2, Irish Repuplic; Tel: +353 (0)1 661 5095 e-mail: praghosa.sdg@pamho.net; www.govindas.ie

London – Govinda's, 10 Soho St, London, W1D 3DL; Tel: +44 (0)20 7437 4928; e-mail: govindas@iskcon-london.org

Nottingham – Govinda's, 7–9 Thurland Street, Nottingham, NG1 3DR; Tel: +44 (0)115 985 9639 e-mail: govindasnottingham@gmail.com; Facebook: www.facebook.com/GovindasNotts

Swansea – Govinda's, 8 Craddock St, Swansea, SA1 3EN; Tel: +44 (0)1792 468469 e-mail: govin_das@hotmail.com

Hare Krishna meetings are held regularly in more than forty towns in the UK.
For more information, contact: ISKCON Reader Services, P.O. Box 730, Watford, WD25 8ZE.
Visit us on the web at www.iskcon.org and for UK info and projects at www.iskconuk.com

Other Countries

Amsterdam, Netherlands — Van Hilligaertstraat 17, Amsterdam 1072 JX; Tel. +31-20-6751404; Fax +31-20-6751405; amsterdam@harekrishna.nl

Brihuega, Spain (New Vraja Mandala) — (Santa Clara) 19411 Brihuega; Tel. +34-949-280436

Budapest, Hungary — Lehel u. 15-17, 1039 Budapest; Tel. +36-1-3910435; Fax +36-1-2423233; info@krisna.hu; www.krisna.hu

Cape Town, South Africa — 17 St Andrews Road, Rondebosch 7700, Cape Town Tel. +27-21-6891060/6861179; iskcon.cape@pamho.net

✦ **Cologne, Germany** — Taunusstrasse 40, 51105 Köln; Tel. +49-221-8303778; restaurant: +49-221-9750323; Fax +49-221-8370485; www.krishna-tempel.de

Copenhagen, Denmark — Skjulhøj Allé 44, 2720 Vanløse; Tel. +45-48-286446; Fax +45-48-287331; iskcon.denmark@pamho.net

Durban, South Africa — 50 Bhaktivedanta Swami Circle, Unit 5 (mail: P.O. Box 56003), Chatsworth 4030; Tel. +27-31-4033328; Fax +27-31-4034429; iskcon.durban@pamho.net

✦ **Durbuy, Belgium** (Radhadesh) — Château de Petite Somme, 6940 Septon-Durbuy; Tel. +32-86-322926; info@radhadesh.com; www.radhadesh.com

Florence, Italy (Villa Vrindavan) — via Scopeti 108, 50026 San Casciano in Val di Pesa (FI); Tel. +39-055-820054; Fax +39-055-828470; isvaripriya@libero.it

Helsinki, Finland — Ruoholahdenkatu 24 D (III krs) 00180 Helsinki; Tel. +358-9-6949879; Fax +358-9-6949837; tapodivyam@krishna.fi; www.krishna.fi

Johannesburg, South Africa — 7971 Capricorn Avenue, (entrance of Nirvana Drive East), Ext 9, Lenasia, Johannesburg; Tel. +27-11-854-1975/7969; iskcon.jh@iafrica.com

Leipzig, Germany — Stöckelstrasse 60, 04347 Leipzig; Tel. +49-34-12348055; sadbhuja@gmx.net; www.krsna-is-cool.de

✦ **Los Angeles, USA** — 3764 Watseka Avenue, 90034; Tel. +1-310-836-2676; Fax +1-310-839-2715; nirantara@juno.com; restaurant: arcita@webcom.com

✦ **Mayapur, India** — Shree Mayapur Chandrodaya Mandir, P.O. Shree Mayapur Dham, Nadia District, W.B. 741 313; Tel. +91-3472-245239; Fax +91-3472-245238; www.mayapur.com

✦ **Mumbai (Bombay), India** — Hare Krishna Land, Juhu 400 049; Tel. +91-22-26206860 Fax +91-22-26205214; www.iskconmumbai.com

✦ **New Delhi, India** — Hare Krishna Hill, Sant Nagar Main Road, East of Kailash, 110 065; Tel. +91-11-26235133; Fax +91-11-26215421; www.iskcondelhi.com; guesthouse: guest.house.new.delhi@pamho.net

New York, USA — 305 Schermerhorn Street, Brooklyn, New York 11217; Tel. +1-718-855-6714; Fax +1-718-875-6127; ramabhadra@aol.com; www.radhagovindanyc.com

Somogyvámos, Hungary — New Vraja-dhama, Fö út. 38., 8699 Somogyvámos; Tel./fax +36-85-340185; info@krisnavolgy.hu; www.krisnavolgy.hu

✦ **Stockholm, Sweden** (city) — Fridhemsgatan 22, 11240 Stockholm; Tel. +46-8-6549002; Fax +46-8-6508813; info@harekrishnastockholm.com; www.harekrishnastockholm.com

Stockholm, Sweden (country) — Radha-Krishna Temple, Korsnäs Gård, 14792 Grödinge; Tel. +46-8-53029800; Fax +46-8-53025062; info@pamho.net; www.krishna.se

Sydney, Australia — 180 Falcon Street, North Sydney, NSW 2060 (mail: P.O. Box 459, Cammeray, NSW 2062); Tel. +61-2-99594558; Fax +61-2-99571893; info@iskcon.com.au; www.iskcon.com.au

✦ **Vrindavan, India** — Krishna-Balaram Mandir, Bhaktivedanta Swami Marg, Raman Reti, Mathura District, 281124; Tel. +91-565-2540021; Fax +91-565-2540053; iskcon.vrndavan@gmail.com; www.iskconvrindavan.com

Zurich, Switzerland — Bergstrasse 54, 8032 Zürich; Tel. +41-1-2623388; Fax +41-1-2623114; kgs@pamho.net; www.krishna.ch

✦ Temples with a restaurant or dining.

This is a partial list of centres. For a full list, please contact one of the above addresses or visit us on the web at www.iskcon.com or www.krishna.com.

To read more about chanting Hare Krishna, Srila Prabhupada and the Beatles, or the blossoming of the Hare Krishna movement in Britain:

When the Sun Shines

The Dawn of Hare Krishna in Britain

by Ranchor Prime

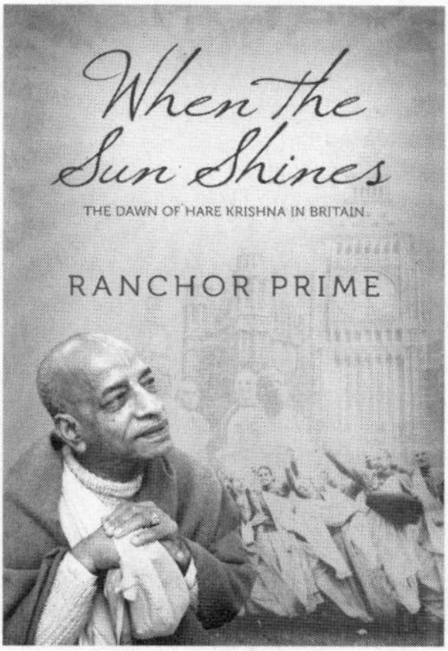

A historical account of the Hare Krishna movement's beginnings and development in Britain, starting with Srila Prabhupada's early days in San Francisco, where the idea of sending six of his young disciples over to England grew, and these disciples' first experiences there – chanting in public and startling the Brits, their serendipitous meetings with various celebrities in the underground, music, and pop culture scene, the historic meeting with the Beatles, and Prabhupada's encouragement and finally arrival. The story takes us from 1967 until Srila Prabhupada's departure in 1977, with a touching account of his last visit to London.

Hardcover, dust jacket, 496 pages, 108 photos,
15.1 × 22.8 cm (9 × 6 in), ISBN 978-1-84599-070-1

Available from:

www.amazon.co.uk
www.blservices.com
shop.bhaktivedantamanor.co.uk
Radha's Boutique, 9–10 Soho Street, London
+44 (0)20 7440 5221

and as an ebook from Amazon, Apple's iBookstore, and the Google Play store.